T0250031

Breaking Out of the Games Industry

Breaking Out of the Games Industry

Matthew M. White

CRC Press
Taylor & Francis Group
Boca Raton   London   New York

CRC Press is an imprint of the
Taylor & Francis Group, an **informa** business

CRC Press
Taylor & Francis Group
6000 Broken Sound Parkway NW, Suite 300
Boca Raton, FL 33487-2742

© 2019 by Taylor & Francis Group, LLC
CRC Press is an imprint of Taylor & Francis Group, an Informa business

No claim to original U.S. Government works

International Standard Book Number-13: 978-0-8153-6006-3 (Paperback)
978-0-8153-6008-7 (Hardback)

Library of Congress Cataloging-in-Publication Data
Names: White, Matthew M., author.
Title: Breaking out of the games industry / Matthew M. White.
Description: Boca Raton, FL : Taylor & Francis, 2019.
Identifiers: LCCN 2018054587| ISBN 9780815360063 (pbk. : alk. paper)	ISBN 9780815360087 (hardback : alk. paper)
Subjects: LCSH: Video games industry--Vocational guidance.	Video games--Design--Vocational guidance.
Classification: LCC HD9993.E452 W55 2019	DDC 794.8023--dc23
LC record available at https://lccn.loc.gov/2018054587

Visit the Taylor & Francis Web site at
http://www.taylorandfrancis.com

and the CRC Press Web site at
http://www.crcpress.com

contents

preface

My first impetus to write this book came from listening to a colleague at Volition describe his past and how he'd ended up working there. He'd gotten his start working on cartridge games back in the 80s and had held over a dozen jobs in half a dozen different cities working on games by that time. While he always had a chipper outlook on the industry, this struck me as uncommon—other professionals surely don't have this much turnover. It's not often your dental hygienist tells you that he's had to move seven times to keep his career—nor your lawyer, your mechanic, your accountant, and so on. While one might reason that entertainment careers are inherently more volatile, digital games are born of technology, and the internet allows us to work from anywhere, for anyone. What then, I thought, caused games in particular to be so volatile?

Unfortunately, neither I nor anyone I know has the answer to that question just yet, and while you'll read a few opinions about it in this book, they are just that, opinions. What mattered most about the conversations I had with this coworker and with the five individuals interviewed in this book, though, were the stories of their careers and the industry that each of them recounted. Like my coworker, more and more folks I spoke to were finding ways to wriggle out of "mainstream" game development and into more freelance, entrepreneurial, "indie" roles. This became part of a larger trend of conversations in my career, at GDC and E3, and beyond.

As more and more of my friends left their cubicles to work on interesting things, go freelance, or start a studio in the Midwest, I too made a change, left my job at PlayStation, and packed up for

Pennsylvania. Whether this is representative of the shifting "gig economy," the games industry particularly, or job dissatisfaction generally, these are the stories of six individuals, one of them me, who made the change from "mainstream" to "indie" development. There's also a roadmap here for how you can make a change, too.

author

Dr. Matthew M. White is a data scientist, game developer, and entrepreneur. He's the managing director of indie game publisher Whitethorn Digital and works in data science in the games industry. With three other professors, he co-developed Penn State University's game development minor, and his AAA game tenure includes Volition, Deep Silver, and PlayStation. He has a Ph.D. in education technology from Memorial University of Newfoundland and still does the odd adjunct class in game development.

introduction

preamble

Before diving right into this book, there are a few laundry items I'd like to get out of the way.

- Game developers are people first, professionals second. This means that when discussing their personal anecdotes, they may say things that offend, have opinions that are unpopular, or otherwise upset you. While I of course made sure these interviews are professional, they have not been edited for content in any way. There is also some profanity, particularly as the interviews drag on. We're foul folks; what can I say?

- This book is designed to read as a guide to making a major change in your game development career and life. It's not here to advance any one "type" of game development as more "real" or "authentic" than any other. It's also not here to single out any company, genre, company size, budget, monetization model, or otherwise. If you're looking for a book to bash what you see as woebegone trends of the industry, this isn't that book, though we'll certainly delve into those topics.

- A large chunk of this book is devoted to the curious, interesting, and odd personal, first-person stories of people who were working in games and decided it was time for a change. Some of these come from a place of positivity and creativity, others, not so much. The stories are told as the developers remember them, and as such are not meant to represent guaranteed facts or statements from either the developers or their current or former companies. Nothing in this book is to be taken as an official statement or stance of any of the companies or entities mentioned herein.

- Neither the opinions of the author nor the opinions of the interviewees represent the official opinion of anyone.

incoherent introductory rant

Somewhere between lunch and sunset, I was having my hair cut in a trailer in a sun baked parking lot in southern California. The company had conveniently arranged for a barber to be brought into the lot once a month so employees could line up and get a chop. God knows, it was the only opportunity you had to do so. Somewhere between your regular (games industry regular) working hours, the grueling commutes, and trying to maintain any semblance of a personal life, your options were pretty much limited to getting a $40 haircut in an aluminum fifth wheel, or swallowing your pride and asking your spouse to just shave your head and buy you a skullcap.

A certain absurdity took me by surprise. The guy wasn't a bad barber. It wasn't a bad trailer. It wasn't even a bad haircut. It was the series of events that led me to sit in the trailer that had me feeling a little spacey. You have a lot of time to think when you're unfortunate enough to have an untalkative barber. Skilled though he may have been, this guy surely did not like to talk. The barber shop is also one of those rare occasions where you can't really access your phone, tucked away under the tarp that catches your hair trimmings. So, in a modern rendition of *The Scream*, I was sitting here, stuck inside my own head with no memes to derail my internal monologue. Save me, doge.

My logic went something like this: the reason I was in the trailer was because I needed a haircut, and getting a haircut myself simply wasn't an option. I was in the office before seven in the morning, and I wasn't out until after five most days. Most barber shops operate in that time frame, so they'd be closed. There were a few others open, but have you ever tried to commute downtown after work in southern California? If you haven't, let's just say getting a haircut was not worth getting home to my wife at three o'clock in the morning. I pondered on.

Eventually, the darker, snarkier part of my brain took hold, as it often does in the postfood three o'clock caffeine lull. Everything about this place, my workplace, was designed so that you never had to leave, or at least so that you wouldn't want to. Food trucks regularly rolled in, the company provided you with snacks and coffee, there were games to play, there were couches to relax on.

Now on the surface, these seem like amenities. Certain "nonsalary perks" any employee should be grateful to have—and that's certainly the case. Believe me, nobody appreciates free coffee more than I do.

There exists, though, a spectrum of employers. Some at the bottom of this spectrum force you to bring your own instant coffee cups, toilet paper, and pencils. On the other hand, some at the top of the spectrum are invested in literally building you a village to live in, deducted right from your salary, effectively closing the loop of ever having you take your cash out of the company. My employers have always been somewhere right in the middle.

After I left the trailer, I started Googling. Other companies, both in my industry and others, did this kind of thing all the time. Bring in a dentist, provide you with an onsite therapist, onsite child care, cafeterias that link directly to your paycheck, education services, professional development services, company stores, even mobile body fat scans and doctor visits.

For whatever momentary malevolent touch of madness that had stricken me, I suddenly saw all of this as a personal invasion. War on my personal life waged by my company, my industry, and the choices I'd made that had led me here.

In that moment, I didn't think of the donuts in the cafeteria as a fun way to reward a week of hard work—suddenly, I thought of them as a very subtle, but very stern, request not to stop for donuts on the way in—in fact, just skip breakfast altogether. The free food and lunch rooms were an invitation to eat quickly and get back to your desk, or if you were feeling ambitious, eat *at* your desk. The board games and couches? Stress relief to offset crunch and long hours. Some places even have a pseudo-bar on site, and you'll regularly find alcohol bottles cluttering games industry desks, played off as being a perk of working in an industry that isn't "uptight," but masking a much less pleasant reality. Even the apples in the cafeteria and the mobile doctors started to feel like a half-baked apology for making you sit in a chair in a cube for 14 hours a day for your entire adult life. An ultimately hollow attempt to clean the conscience of a middle manager somewhere watching her workforce gradually turn gray and plump.

Every little "service" given to me, in that moment, felt like another erosion of my life that had happened so gradually I hadn't noticed it at all. My personal moments—silly freedoms, like moments at the barber shop, half-intelligible open-mouthed conversations at the dentist, hell, even venting at therapy, were all available to me through my workplace. I started to hyperventilate inside of my climate-controlled carpet cube.

In reality, and I'm sure you'll be relieved to hear, neither this realization nor this book are about the barber in the parking lot. Rather, both are about a certain discordance between my goals and where I'd somehow ended up, and how both I and others have managed to wriggle our way out.

Like most people working in games, I started as a starry-eyed, ninja-turtles-underwear-clad little kid, plopped on my butt on the floor of my living room, dominating the television set with my NES and *The Legend of Zelda*, among others. Something was just so uncannily amazing about games. My parents played games only a little bit in the late 70s, I think. My dad had an Atari 2600, and I remember playing *Ms. Pac Man* on it with him a bit when he was still around. My mother was more interested in games like *Jeopardy!* that tested your knowledge or puzzle-solving skills. Between playing games with mom and my friends and eating sugary cereal in my underpants, it was a good time to be alive.

As I got older, the interest never waned. In high school, I wrote letters to a few game companies I really admired, back when people still did that, asking how to get into the games industry by any means necessary. This is what I wanted to do with my life, and it's still what I want to do with my life.

Shockingly, Squaresoft responded to me, a then-13-year-old kid in Nova Scotia. They had their artists offer some career advice, as well as some programmers, and even the person who wrote the letter wished me well. It was awesome. It even got me a nickname— "Squaresoft boy"—probably the only flattering nickname I have had to date.

Somewhere between being a wide-eyed kid who wanted to make video games and sitting in a cubicle baking under fluorescent lights and itching from my company-sponsored haircut, I lost my way. Even the work I was doing had started to drift decidedly into the *make-more-money* realm, instead of the *make-better-games* one. My personal sense of what games *are* was at conflict with the work I was doing every day.

I started to question everything about the *California-as-endgame* mentality I had nurtured about my life and this industry. It was in that moment that I decided, somewhat brazenly, that I wouldn't be renewing my lease, and I wouldn't be renewing my contract.

Soon I started questioning other things about my life:

- Why am I paying $3500 a month to live in a small apartment in the middle of a stinking desert?
- Why do I think it's normal that my backyard is on fire?
- Why do I tolerate an up-to-two-hour commute to go less than 15 miles?
- Why is it $60 to take my wife to a movie?
- Why is *everything* so expensive?
- Why am I simultaneously making six figures and completely broke?
- Why is the air quality so atrocious?
- Why do I spend 10 or more hours a day working on things that either don't interest me or actively repulse me? *This wasn't what I signed up for.*

I had published an indie game—*Beans: The Coffee Shop Simulator.* It wasn't exactly flying off the shelves, but the fact that it sold at all was all the proof I needed. I spent my entire yearly bonus moving my wife and me across the country to northwestern Pennsylvania. I secured a remote job doing more or less the same thing I was doing for the company. Soon, 80 percent of my free time shifted over to my next game project, a much bigger one this time. I was exercising creative control, working on something I loved, and drinking a $2 beer in a bar five minutes from my $80,000 home where the bartender knew my name and the air tasted like something other than exhaust fumes. My indie adventure was just beginning.

If anything I've said here sounds like your life, maybe it's time for you to break out, too? Read on!

making video games

I'm sure you're not reading this book to hear about my life story, and this certainly isn't meant to be my autobiography, so I'll try my hardest to keep this chapter very brief. In short, if you read it and it sounds anything like your life, I hope it will inspire you to flip to the interviews and the how-to guide in the rest of this book and maybe make your own move.

Pretty much for as long as I can remember, I've always wanted to make video games. Growing up in the 90s, you had all kinds of opportunities to go to game shops, rent games, play games with friends, go to arcades, play *Pokemon* in school ... games and skateboards were pretty much my childhood. There weren't really many game programs at universities and schools yet, at least none that I knew of. Certainly, you had the vague idea of what making a game was: someone needed to know how to draw, someone else needed to know how to play music, somebody needed to know something or other about computers. Somehow, you put all of that together and it just became fun—there was some writing and storytelling in there, too, I thought.

I ended up with a weird mishmash of talents and skills. I played some music after school, did some 3D modeling, learned everything I could about computers and technology (on my handy-dandy Windows 3.1 and DOS machines), and even figured out a bit about writing, screenplays, drama, and fiction.

Where I grew up, there wasn't exactly a market for video game development. The internet was only recently becoming available for average folks, and being on an island on Canada's east coast didn't exactly provide you with ample networking opportunities. I figured I needed a backup plan, a second career that I also enjoyed, but my primary focus—I told myself—would be the video games.

Ten years later, I had most of a Ph.D. in education technology studying learning in games and no real idea how I was going to get into the games industry, or even how I'd gotten there. On a wild longshot, I applied for an International Game Developers Assocation (IGDA) scholarship to attend Game Developers Conference (GDC). Maybe someone knew what to do with a jack-of-all-trades background and a guy studying how people learn from tutorials in *World of Warcraft*, because I certainly didn't.

As it turns out, someone *did* know what to do with me. The newly formed Games User Research SIG of the IGDA was an outlet for other people who were studying the player and her mind. Over the years, this would later blossom into a much larger study of players generally, including disciplines like user experience, UX design, market research, analytics, and telemetry.

That basically did it for me. I'd be a player insights professional and learn as much as I could about cognitive psychology, user interface design, user experience, data collection and analysis, and so on.

The Startup Phase, or, "What the Hell Am I Doing?!"

While the GDC trip, the networking, the generosity and goodwill of the IGDA, and an unlimited supply of youthful energy were certainly positive, they didn't solve a key problem for me—namely, I lived on an island in the middle of the sea, and there wasn't a games industry anywhere near me. Couple that with the fact that user research was only recently emerging as a discipline, and this didn't exactly lay blueprints for fast success. In my estimation, I had two options going forward—I could either move to a large, metropolitan city that housed game developers on the bleeding edge, like San Francisco, or I could run a startup and sell to those individuals in the games industry who hadn't yet adopted user research. A combination of bravery, boldness, youthful arrogance, and stupidity led me to do the latter. Several times. All things told, I ran three startups, all of which failed at one point or another, but all of which taught me something.

Startup #1: Potential Design Software

I wasn't sure what to call it. We went with "Potential Design," because my friend Stephen and I thought it sounded intelligent and vague. I have since learned that being vague does not actually guarantee you customers, and making it unclear what you're actually selling or doing only seems to make you a profit if you're Apple. The core business model was pretty simple. Sell insight and development services to local, smaller companies, then make games ourselves. Like most people, however, I underestimated how much actual effort, planning, and time actually went into making a game. ***Ridiculously***. The company folded after about a year, with mostly just prototypes under our belts and only a handful of small clients.

Startup #2: Pragmatic Gaming Laboratory

This time, we took a run at it in earnest. I put most of my development ambitions aside for the time being and decided to focus entirely on the insights portion. We went whole hog here, and my friend Matt and I purchased some beefy development machines to run client builds and some very expensive (at the time) biometric measuring equipment. To this day, one of the most irritating old pains remains the nearly 10 grand I spent on things that can now be made for 50 bucks with an Arduino and a soldering iron.

Adding salt to that wound, turns out that user research has now all but abandoned biometrics by and large—generally speaking, it's much more effort for only minimal gains. I didn't know this at the time, though, and admittedly the idea of hooking a customer's players up to things that monitor them physically and psychologically was definitely a compelling selling point—it all seemed very "sciency." We took some lessons on business, bought some books, got some sales coaching, made up some documents, and booked our first major games industry trade fair—Tokyo Game Show. Lesson #1 here—don't try to sell something extremely complicated in a language you don't really speak all that well. Do *you* know how to say "electroencephalography" in Japanese? I'm not sure I'm even saying it right in English. Regardless, we did get some clients, but honestly were so overwhelmed that someone wanted our services that we didn't know what to do to actually sell them. We worked on a few projects before shutting the company down after about a year and a half of operations.

Startup #3: Snow Day Games

This time around, I figured we needed more revenue, faster—and an outside supporting body to help us get that revenue. The previous two startups were funded entirely with our own money, but this time, I partnered with a government startup and incubator in Prince Edward Island and moved on over. I'd teach or at least do research at the local university and make games half time while hiring some other full-time workers. I picked up scrum and agile training, and went to town on starting a business in a more legitimate setting. This was during the beginning of the "app development" bubble on the early iPhone. We published two or three games, depending on how you define "game."

First was *Yo Momma Generator!*—a masterpiece of high-brow humor that used a dictionary file and a short Objective C program to generate random "yo momma so ..." jokes by using a scan of the English dictionary and sorting words into types (adjective, noun, and so on). It was something I came up with one night while drinking heavily. Because it didn't take into account whether the words fit into the sentence, the nonsense it churned out was actually pretty amusing. If you wanted to hear a half-assed hip-hop beat, see a microphone in front of a spotlighted brick wall, and press a button to get classics like "yo momma so tumescent she recapitulates purple decadence," this was the app for you. We sold it for $0.99 and it moved about a thousand copies.

With art talent like that, is it any wonder I'm not a millionaire yet?

Second, we made a game called *Fly vs. Car.* We partnered with Child's Play, a charity I still admire and encourage you to visit, and pledged to give half of our profits to them after the game came out. This was much more of a *game* than the previous app. You played the part of a little fly that flew back and forth by tilting the iPhone around, trying not to get smashed by oncoming cars. The more you could avoid, the higher the score, and so on. This predated the iPhone achievement stuff, so we used a third-party program called OpenFeint. Unfortunately, we spent *insanely* on the soundtrack, trying to copy the then-overwhelmingly-popular *Angry Birds* sound. We also learned the hard way that when you have money, a million people will show up to encourage you to spend it. As a result, contractors and consultants sapped a huge amount of our working capital. To that end, we *never actually made a profit on this game* and didn't make our money back on development, resulting in a whopping $0 donation to Child's Play, something I still feel guilty about. In any case, the game sold another thousand or so units.

I actually still have fun playing this.

Finally, we made *Ninja Junk Punch*. God, **what a stupid idea this was**. We had this friend, Chris. Chris was a great guy, but Chris smoked a *lot* of weed. It was basically all he did. When Chris got high, he'd spend his time flicking around on his iPhone. My then–business partner Jeff said, "What if ... what if we made a game for stoners who just sit there baked and play with their iPhones? That market has to be huge." I agreed with that—baked college kids definitely weren't going anywhere. The next part ... "What if we got Chris to get really, really baked and come up with the idea for the game? By stoners, for stoners, right?" Seemed logical.

It wasn't.

Ninja Junk Punch, originally titled *Ninja Dick Punch* until we realized there was no way that was ever going to get on iTunes, was a *Punch Out!* clone in which players played the part of Trent the lumberjack. Trent had been out tending to his lumberly duties when he returned home only to find his wife sleeping with a ninja. In order to rectify the situation, players have to punch the ninjas repeatedly in the genitals until they submit. The player then uncovers a massive, worldwide conspiracy involving ninjas, all of whom need their genitals punched in.

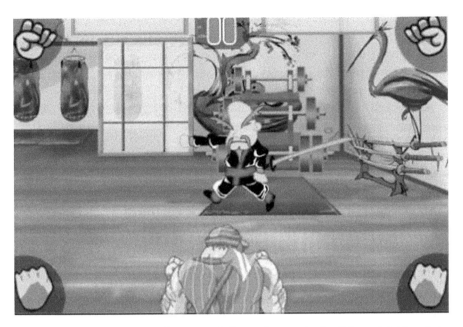

This old man has wronged you, and the only way to fix it is a right hook to the testicles.

As I sit here writing this, a grown man on a work trip in Montreal who's worked on a dozen or more AAA and indie games, I'm still shaking my head at myself for this one. Then again, I later worked for Volition and spent my time beating people with a six-foot dildo-on-a-stick. Maybe it's just the games industry.

The game featured training minigames, fun artwork, and an original soundtrack. It was pretty good, I think, but was panned for unresponsive gameplay and choppy controls, which was a fair criticism. The game did OK in terms of sales, but once again, the bills became more than we were making. We were in the middle of making another game, *Fist of the Beast King*, where you smashed a giant fist down on little pixel cities to grind them into dust, when the company ran too far into the red, and we had to shut the doors for a third time.

struggling with legitimacy

Nina Freeman hosted the IGF awards in 2017. She said, referring to developers who are nontraditional and who may not think of themselves as "real" developers: "Trust me honey, you're just as real as the rest of us." This is probably something I wish I had heard back in 2009, and not nearly a decade later.

After closing the doors on the last startup, I got a divorce, lived in Japan for a while, worked on tutorials for *World of Warcraft* as part of my Ph.D. thesis, and took a position at Penn State teaching game development. In my free time, I was working on independent and student games, helping them publish things in a safer environment than I had experienced. We built a game lab on campus, and I was taking students to GDC every year. Occasionally, I would spend my summers contracting doing data analytics and user research with some AAA companies, and occasionally local indies. I also taught game development to children at a summer camp. This was, all things considered, a pretty sweet gig.

Still, the struggle to feel like I'd "made it" and that I had become a "real game developer" was definitely always hanging over my head. After about a year or two of battling with that, I republished *Fly vs. Car* on Android. It felt good to just be making and selling games again. It wasn't too long after this that I took an offer from Volition to work full time as a data scientist in Champaign, IL.

the big leagues

My first "real" gig was with Volition. I worked first on analytics for *Saints Row IV*, then eventually did the full data science stack on *Agents of Mayhem*, supported by an awesome data engineer. I also spent some time pinch hitting analytics for other Deep Silver titles like *Homefront: The Revolution.*

This was great. It was pretty much everything I wanted. Awesome game development studio, flex hours, lots of wonderful in-office amenities, friends and colleagues to work with, and lots of different projects every single day. I learned so much here, because not only did I have to solve new and unique analytics problems nearly every day, but I also got lots of downtime during early development to take courses, do professional development, and more.

For personal and quality-of-life reasons, Champaign wasn't the best city for me. It's a fine place, it just didn't jive with the kinds of things my wife and I liked to do. While this certainly wasn't a dealbreaker, it started to grate on us after a while. On top of that, our current project was slowly entering into what can commonly be described as *development Hell*. Deadlines were soaring by, project parameters and scope were changing, and so on. If you're in games, you're probably pretty familiar with what this feels like.

As both of these factors started to increase friction in my day to day, I found myself at GDC, not actively looking for new work, but certainly not opposed to entertaining the idea if it came my way. Turns out there was a bit of a data bubble happening, and lots of work did, in fact, come my way. After entertaining a few offers, I ended up deciding that I'd now be working for PlayStation in sunny SoCal.

As far as I knew, this was it—I'd finish my career here. I was working for a major publisher in a big city, living the game dev dream. This is about the part where we end up in the barber shop in the trailer from the introduction. The commutes were long, the work longer, and the quality of life rapidly started to decline. Eventually, I got to a point where I wasn't really ever working on games anymore, just spreadsheets, projections, and A/B tests on dozens of titles, all day, every day. Bizarrely, as I'd entered one of the biggest and best game development companies on the planet, I'd gotten about as far from working on games as I'd ever been.

The itch to make games persisted, though, so I did what I would consider **step one on getting on your own path to game dev nirvana**—I made a game.

my (sort of) first little indie game

Everyone has a hobby. My hobby just turns out to be exactly the same thing as my job. I'm kind of a one-trick pony sometimes. In any case, after about a year or two of working, I launched *Beans: The Coffee Shop Simulator*. I want to be clear—this is a complete #hobbydev game. It's not a masterpiece, it's full of bugs, and the art is of questionable quality. Regardless, I had a great time making game design decisions and putting sweat into making a product. There's a certain indelible feeling of value that comes from the act of making and completing a thing.

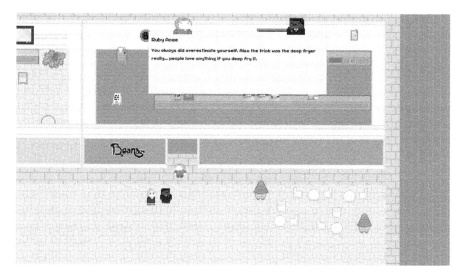

It's true.

Beans is a coffee shop simulator. You play as Ruby Acee, disillusioned former engineer and lawyer who's been forced to move home after getting fired from her job in the big city (for "allegedly" giving the boss's son a piledriver). By a series of completely unreasonable circumstances, Ruby inherits a massive fortune, provided she can emerge victorious in a series of trials that involve opening coffee shops and squaring off against drones, malevolent chickens, and poorly drawn, unauthorized impersonations of Gordon Ramsay.

The game is a goofy thing that was an outlet for my frustrations at my job. You'll find it full of stabs at all kinds of things kicking around the games industry. Maybe someday I'll give a talk about gamedev as therapy for occupational burnout; more likely, I'll be too burned out to write the talk.

The game launched in late summer of 2017, a little after I'd had my barber-shop-trailer moment. While it wasn't breaking any sales records, *it made money*. We made back our development expenses several times over. That was a bit of a sign for me—I could do this myself. I didn't need to spend another second in a carpeted cube. I could get away from my commute, buzzing fluorescent lights, crunch time, and "crying rooms" once and for all.

breaking out to break in

I was ready to move with nothing lined up, but as luck would have it, I took an *amazing* remote job with a company that allowed me to continue doing data and analytics work from wherever I wanted. I used my yearly bonus to send all of my belongings to Pennsylvania in the back of a shipping truck, and got in the car with my wife and drove a few thousand miles.

We moved to Erie, Pennsylvania. We had lived here previously, and the city has a lot of great game developers that are just starting to bud. No central group exists to get them all in one building.

As of the time of writing, I'm laying drywall in my startup office, putting together Whitethorn Digital, a publisher, developer, and incubator that's going to bring these folks together and help them make great games. Just like craft beer, I think there's a future for games in this city and in thousands of other cities around the world—not just in three or four cities making big beer or big games!

I'm going to spend some time interviewing other people who left traditional game development to forge their own paths. I hope you'll find some inspiration in their stories, and maybe that will be the catalyst you need to leave your cube, too.

how did they do it?

I'd like to spend a pretty significant amount of time in this book talking to other more experienced game developers about their moves. Not everyone in this book completely left the games industry, went indie, flipped out, and moved across the country, or even had a negative experience. The one thing that binds these folks together is that they all decided it was time to leave a "traditional" development role—that is, one working on a large AAA team making a flagship-sized product— to something else, whether that be consulting, indie development, or leaving the games industry altogether. Hopefully, in their stories, you can find some hope and guidance for making your own move.

Ben Serviss, formerly THQ*ICE

I met Ben at GDC 2009. He was mentoring younger games industry professionals (and was in fact my mentor). At the time, he was with THQ*ICE, working on localization and project management. Ben has since left the games industry under what many would consider pretty unfortunate circumstances, but he considers himself all the better for it.

MW: Hey—thanks again for taking the interview. Introduce yourself please!

BS: Sure. Ben Serviss. I was working in the game industry for like 8 or 10 years off and on, and now I'm a web developer and extremely part-time game developer.

MW: OK great. So throughout, I'm going to ask you a bunch of questions that are little probes about your career, why you left, what you do now, that sort of thing. At any time, you can of course omit anything you're uncomfortable sharing, or that has an NDA or anything like that, and of course you can feel free to plug anything that you are working on.

So number one, can you give me a little career rundown? Sort of where you were, and the kinds of things you worked on that you're able to share?

BS: So I started in 2004. Um, it was a combination of writing for this new site called mygamer.com, which was like … they didn't pay anybody, so it was more of, "Hey, I want to be involved in games in some kind of way" … and that was a good first step. So I did that. At the same time, I joined the IGDA chapter in New Jersey just to meet other people that were interested in game development because I knew I wanted to be involved in making games but didn't really know how to do that or what I would even be good at doing. So those are the biggest things in terms of just meeting people and contacts and getting an idea of what I should be doing through the IGDA. By writing for the website, I got to go to GDC on a press pass, which was really cool. It was like a whole lot of, you know, just new things and the scope of what the game industry actually was, as opposed to just reading magazine articles about it.

MW: The press pass … it gives you access to all kinds of stuff that you would otherwise not have at GDC as well.

BS: Yeah. So that was huge. And that was in 2005. Also, in college, I worked for a tiny two-person game studio. One person was in Binghamton, New York, which is where I went to college, and the other person was in New Zealand and they had this online studio just making like text-based games, and I'd work for them doing some writing. So that was an interesting first step there. And then from there, through people I'd met at GDC, I got referred for a contract job and then did that for a while, and then after that I got referred for my first full-time job, which was associate producer at Saber Interactive in New Jersey.

So I was there. I worked there for about a year and a half, and then I left after we finished *TimeShift*. Then I moved to

LA and I was working as a product manager for THQ*ICE, who were doing free to play. It was after I was there for about a year that I was at that point where I was just really burned out with games because the hours were crazy, and the crunching, and the time zones were really bad. Saber's main office was in Russia, so we were working on Russia time. And then at THQ, the developer of the game was in Korea and we were in LA, and it was a joint venture between THQ and a company in China. So we were working on Asia time, and it was just like crazy hours to begin with. Plus the time difference for us.

Hectic insanity, but I guess it's the typical kind of game stuff. After about a year of that, I completely burned out and said, "I don't want to be doing this. I can't, I can't do this right now. I'm not too sure what I want to do, but it can't be this."

Yeah. So then that was like 2010, and my sister was in Portland, Oregon. So I moved up there and then we set up like a family business because my parents had moved there, too. So my dad is an editor, my mom's a writer, my sister has a film degree, and I knew enough about production and games and software development and a little bit of web stuff. So we made this online news site; it was like a family business, but that didn't go too well either.

So at that point I was thinking, well, I don't really know what to do next or at all, but I just wanted to come back to New York. My parents came back to New York and my sister went to Boston, and when they got back, I wasn't … I was still kind of like gun shy from working in games. So I had two interviews; I had an interview with Arkadium, who were making mobile games and casual games, and I think also some work-for-hire stuff. I interviewed with them for a contract writing position, and some other stuff. And then on the other side, I had an interview with a newspaper to do social media essentially, and I got an offer from the newspaper.

So I did that first. And then I got an offer to do some contract work for Arkadium. And then after a few weeks of that, they made me an offer for a full-time thing, but I was still kind of a little wary of games, so I just stuck with doing contract work for them. It was after I was there for a few years at the newspaper that I left and I tried to do freelance game design stuff, just to give that a shot. I did that for about a year.

Then I also met a bunch of people at the first Global Game Jam I went to in 2013. I met a like-minded group of people, and we had a ton of fun. And then we ended up forming an indie game company and we formed a studio and we worked on that for like two or three years.

We were really trying hard to make the studio work, but it was just a lot of effort. It's really hard to make it work. And I was still trying to get all the contract work and stuff to work out ... and it was really not ... it didn't look like a sustainable kind of thing.

So at that point, I think this is 2014, I went to the Flatiron School, which is a web development boot camp, a three-month program. It's a full-time immersive program. I came out of there and I interned at Shapeways, which is a 3D printing company. And then from there I got a job at my current company, which is BeenVerified, and they handle background checks and public records information. So this is thoroughly outside of games at this point.

I've also been doing some game freelance stuff, though. I wrote a game for Choice of Games—they do choose-your-own-adventure games for mobile and Steam. So that took maybe a year and a half, two years to write and develop. And I did do a fair amount of other contract work, too. It just wasn't, there wasn't enough of it to always have to have a reliable source of income and to have stability at that point. I liked working in games, but I wanted to not have to worry about what I was going to be doing for money and living. So, doing web stuff has been really good because now I have a better idea of all the logic and coding that go into games, but you know, there's more stability, so I'm not worrying about what the hell I'm going to be doing with my life.

And now it's easier to kind of dip in and out of game stuff. So I haven't really been doing too much, but I do some work with the Death by Audio Arcade, which is a group of indie game developers and arcade cabinet fabricators. I was part of the initial group that formed in 2013 because the main guy, Mark Kleback, was living and working at Death by Audio, which was a music venue slash DIY kind of space in Brooklyn, and he wanted to get more involved in games. So he collected a whole bunch of indie games people and people that were down to do some weird arcade/interactive projects, and we've still been doing projects since. We've toured around a lot to places like the Smithsonian American Art Museum and Maker Faire. We've also got a whole section at MAGFest. So that group's been doing a lot of cool stuff and I'm still tangentially involved.

I still can't quit games completely. It's been impossible. I'm still looking at Kotaku and everything and keeping up with what's going on. I finally got a PS4 and I'm like playing more games, so in that way getting a little bit outside of working in games has been good for just me playing them.

MW: That's actually the next question—when did you first know you wanted to work in and around games? Just briefly.

BS: I just always played them and really liked them. We had the original NES growing up, so that was our baseline ... and just to kind of like ... the sense of being able to just get lost playing a game, especially a single-player game with a good narrative. Your imagination had to meet what the game was trying to do because the graphics were so bad. But it was when I got *Metal Gear Solid* and played that, because it was so cinematic and it really drew you in and the narrative was just so sure of itself and kind of nuts. Like I really had no idea that was even possible. When I played that, I really wanted to somehow be a part of it.

MW: I think that was *Final Fantasy VII* for me, you know, at some point I sat and I realized that I was playing a game for like 18 hours a day and was just like, oh my God, I'm on summer break from high school and I haven't left the house, what am I doing with my life? My thumbs are blue and yeah ... no, I completely understand that.

So, when do you think was the moment where you wanted to move out of the total kind of grind of being in the games industry full time? You mentioned a few issues that were sort of grating, like the time zones, the crunch, things like that. Particularly, if you had any "red flag" kind of a moment in time where you sort of knew that this was not the right path, I'd love to hear about that.

BS: Yeah ... I don't talk about this too much at this point. *pause* It's been awhile and I like the fact that you're doing this book as kind of like a cautionary thing. Like, just be aware of what you're getting into.

MW: Yeah, I certainly don't want when I write it, I definitely don't want to come off like "fuck the games industry" because that is definitely not what I'm going for. It's just ... what I'm trying to do is chronicle what I see as a real shift, like people going to craft beer, a change that's happening in the games industry from Budweiser, Coors, and Miller to a whole tapestry of really interesting and very different things happening around the entire country. The reasons that somebody sitting and mechanically pouring 20 tons of barley into a vat every day is like, "man, I just love beer—why the hell am I doing this?" And then going back to their hometown and buying a mash tun and making their own. Uh, and that's, that's kind of the shift that I think is really interesting.

BS: Well, I'll tell you when I was at my second full-time job, because the hours were, were so crazy ... I think I would get into work at like 11 and then come home at 2 or something.

MW: Like, AM? 11 AM to 2 AM?

BS: Yeah, it's brutal because it felt like we were always chasing this thing that we couldn't figure out exactly how to do. So that was going on for months and then I was driving to work on the Interstate, I think it was north on the 405, then west on the 101. Anyway, It was like up north [of LA] ... anyway, I fell asleep at the wheel and I hit a truck on the left rear wheel and spun out to the left ... and there were no other cars there, and my car came to a stop just short of the divider. I got out and I was like, oh, OK, I've never done that before ever. And just like the fact that ... I was fine. I had one stitch because my head hit the airbag and that was, that was like, it.

... *pause*

So, after that happened, I was like, OK, this is not gonna work.

MW: Wow.

My experiences, mine were more existential than I guess yours was. Yours was really literally existential in the sense of: you may not exist if you keep doing it. OK, wow.

Following that up is difficult ... But um, well, the next question I usually ask people is: What was "missing" from your work life? Like ... what do you think now that presumably what you do is a little more enjoyable and fulfilling ... what's here at this job that wasn't there at your old job?

BS: The thing that's missing? Now?

MW: Sorry. The thing that was missing besides the ... well, obviously you were being worked to death, but typically ... so I'll leave this question here and I'll sort of segue for a second.

I leave this question in here for people who don't have an "I fell asleep at the wheel and nearly died" moment, because oftentimes the reason they leave is a little more soft. It's kinda like, you know, for example, monetization, people will sometimes say "at some point I stopped making games and started making money." This was certainly the case for me— everything I was doing every day was really like, how do we pull another $5 out of people? How do we pull another five cents out of every million people, whatever. And it got to this really ... like the mindset was really not where I wanted it to be at all. Not at all why I got into games.

MW, cont'd: So ... I mean if I was working for a bank or MasterCard or something doing that kind of financial work, I'd make triple what I do now ... but you get into games because what you do is something you really care about, you sort of feel that mission kind of deal.

It's a soft thing like teaching where you know you're going to be paid really poorly, but you love what you do. Um, and so I think at some point for me, the thing that was missing was that I didn't feel like I was working on games anymore. I felt like I was working on a very complex monetary Skinner box, like a Pachinko machine or something. And I really hated that ... and so it's that kind of thing. But if you don't have an answer to that one, that's fine. It's just sort of here to let you kind of introspect about the job. And the differences between where you thought it was going to be and where it actually ended up.

BS: There's an element of that for me too, though, because when I was working at THQ, it was like trying to try to figure out how to do free to play because no one at THQ had done that yet, and it got to the same kind of point where we were just asking,

"How can we get people to buy more costumes?" or whatever. And it was less about making a game, which was the whole point of doing this. It was a little harder to tell that this was happening, because my first jobs out of college were at game studios. So I didn't really have any other non–game industry experience to compare to my THQ experience.

So it was just like your entire existence because you were always ... there was always some kind of deadline going on.

BS, cont'd: And you'd constantly be fighting this battle and ... you can't ever actually win. I'd make plans for vacations and things, and then some kind of crazy deadline would come up or something would happen and I'd just have to cancel it all.

I guess that would make more sense if you had a more important kind of job like working in the military or, you know, something where lives were at stake, but we're making hats for fuck's sake. People are like, we're making the gun better to shoot digitally. It's not, it shouldn't *pause* ... it shouldn't have this kind of effect on people's lives.

MW: Right. You know, I have this conversation occasionally with people. In statistics, there's a question about a concept called p-value that comes up a lot of the time; it's a number that you use to measure mathematical certainty, and in certain college classes, they teach you a particular value of it that you always want to search for. But in games we accept a much looser value. And usually the reason for that is because if we're wrong, nobody dies. Right? Like, so it's exactly what you're talking about. The "criticality" of it all is very low.

So the next bit is on logistics. When you decided it was time to be like, OK, this isn't for me anymore. It's kind of like what you did, how you did it, the actual steps of like, "How did I transition out of that life?" What were the blow-by-blow steps you took to get out of game development?

BS: Yeah, well it was kind of hard because I started this whole process of coming out of this craziness and the car accident. So it wasn't a well-laid-out business plan or anything. Something that did help in the beginning was when I was talking to my boss about it, I mentioned that I could work remotely for a bit and he was OK with that. So that's what I did for a little bit to start with, which just helped me make the transition a little more easily. But outside of that, I had some savings that I really relied on for a while just to kind of figure out what to do with my life now because I was so into games and then to be ... to be that into it and then to get that thoroughly, not rejected, but just like almost destroyed by it ...

BS, cont'd: I didn't really know what to do; what I was supposed to do next? My only experience working in games had been so extremely destructive. So processing that was rough. And then trying to start up another business for the wrong reasons was a bad idea, too. So it was really rough coming out of that and trying to figure out what to do next. But then after that I regrouped and tried to reformulate things based on stuff that I knew. So I knew New York, I knew online news and social media and things related to that.

BS, cont'd: I was just trying to get back on firm footing and figure out exactly how I could engage with game development as a career, because I still liked it. I just didn't know how to get involved in it without horrible things happening, I needed to spend some time getting back to some stability. I spent some time working at the newspaper and then from there started evaluating options and then tried some other things like freelancing, that and some other contract stuff. I did a startup thing, and then at that point realized that what I wanted most was more stability, so that's why I went to web development and kind of pivoted away from games ... but even then, it's still close enough to game development because of the software angle, so it felt like it was related. I didn't move to web development with a plan of learning how to be a programmer and then coming back to games later; it was more like I just needed a little bit more stability in my life and needed some time to figure out if there was more I was going to do with games.

MW: That's perfect. When you had that conversation with your boss, I think that's kind of one of these things that a lot of people dread—going in and saying, "Hey, I'm leaving." How was that?

BS: Well, compared to the car accident ...

MW: Yeah, good point. That's terrifying. You kind of have a little bit of a unique situation here because I feel like most people work themselves up and are worried about talking to their bosses and end up not doing it, but when something like that car accident happens, you get a real kick in the pants, you know? You know right then and there.

BS: My boss was really good about it. He was very understanding and he was … he was a solid guy about it.

MW: Yeah. Actually when I left, my boss was surprisingly OK with it as well. I thought he was going to absolutely kill me, seriously. I was really scared, but he was super chill.

So the new venture you've talked about … any regrets on the change? Would you go back to games full-time if you could?

BS: I just can't justify it. First of all, I know that my experience isn't everyone's experience. I got my first job at the same time a bunch of my friends got their first game jobs and they've also had hard, weird jobs and crunch and everything, but they all kind of agree that I had the weirdest, most intense experience, and it's kind of a shame because if I had a better experience at other companies that, you know, weren't under crazy pressure, whatever it was, maybe I would still be doing it. But I don't see the need to potentially subject myself to those kinds of hours and that kind of lifestyle of basically being "on call." Especially because my situation now is I'm working remotely for my company.

BS, cont'd: I'm in Columbus because my girlfriend is going to grad school here until she's done with her program. I don't know what we're going to do next. So because there's the opportunity to be a remote person in web development, you know it's just a lot more in demand at this point. So it's easier to get other jobs. For game development, you have to move all the time to find a job. The opportunities that doing web development opens up, the more relaxed kind of livable lifestyle … the pay is generally higher than in games. So, I wouldn't go back to games full-time. If anything, I would do side projects or do game development on my time on my own terms.

MW: Yeah. Again, that's another interesting thing that a few folks that I'm talking to have started to do is small, not even "indie" development, they're almost calling it hobby-dev or a bit like home brewing.

OK—Sorry, you do not have to answer this question directly or obliquely, but here goes. How's your financial situation now? Do you think it's gotten easier? Harder?

BS: Yeah, it's way better. That is as a result of both the pay and the quality of life. It's better in every possible dimension.

MW: Other folks have told me how every minute they weren't at work they would spend their money like crazy because they were trying to squeeze their lives into four or five hours awake and not at work. So one of the things that people talked about so far that's been kind of unexpected is like, yeah, the salary was better, but also now I'm not spending like a thousand bucks a month on drinking or things like that to try to cope.

BS: Or ordering lunch all the time or ordering dinner because I have no time to cook.

MW: Right. Yeah. That's the thing.

The third part is more about your life now. So the work you do on games now is just on your own time, as opposed to a more "traditional" role in the games industry. Since you've made that change, what do your daily worries look like now as compared to your daily worries at any one of the studios? Minus the driving off the road asleep part of course.

BS: I'm able to actually have my own life and not feel bad about it. Because when I was working at the other gaming companies, we were always wrestling with "How do we make this thing better?" "How do we improve this thing?" "How do we make this good to begin with?" "What's the timeline going to be like for that?" "This thing is in trouble right now. We've got to fix that." Just constantly, it just never stopped. And then I would get home and I would be exhausted and I wouldn't even really know what to do. Like I don't really want to play another game. I've just been looking at games all day and I'm too tired to do anything.

But now I work normal hours. I worked late once or twice in the three years that I've been at this company and nobody, like, forced me to do it or just kind of, you know, suggested I do it. It's just a way better quality of life.

MW: Ah yea, getting "voluntold." That's come up in several of my conversations with developers. It's like … no one's actually telling you they will fire you if you don't stay 14 hours a day. But we're certainly implying it strongly, or bragging about our "work ethic" in interviews.

Clearly you think your life has improved, but do you think eventually you would have gotten to this point anyway, where you just moved away to a different career out of games, had you not had the car accident?

BS: I'm really surprised at how things turned out. I think if I hadn't had as severe an experience and if I'd worked at companies that weren't up against crazy deadlines, there's a decent chance I would still be working in games.

I mean, I may have stuck it out longer. I'm sure that it would have happened, but I don't know if it's inevitable. It's hard to say. I don't think it was. I don't think it was 100% that I was going to switch into something out of games. Because it seems to be the norm that conditions [in the game industry] are bad.

Hey, you know, it isn't so good that the hours are crazy. And yea, it's like a real hit on your ability to do other things with your life. At some point I guess I realized that … wait a minute, something needs to change. Maybe, maybe it would've taken longer.

MW: You know, this is kind of off the script a little bit, but an interesting question that came to me while we've been talking about this is that … there's often a lot of moving and turnover. You know, you'll go to GDC one year. You'll speak to someone you know really well and you'll say, oh, how's company A? And they'll say, oh, I'm actually at company B, and then you'll see them the next year and hey, how's company B and oh, I'm actually at company C now. And that turnover speed is really quite astronomical. Do you think to some extent there might be something to that? Where you're kind of looking for something that isn't maybe so easy to find in a new job? Sort of constantly always looking at the greener grass?

BS: Well, yeah, I think that's because no job or company or anything is perfect in games. The issues are really clear when you're experiencing them. If you are working at a studio that has a really great track record and a great reputation, but there's three things or two things that you hate about it, then you start thinking, oh, what if I went to this other place? Maybe it'll be a bigger company and things will be better, or a smaller company and I'll have more control or freedom or something. Plus, it's just the nature of it. If you work at a game company, you're probably a gamer ... So you're trying to think like, all right, if I could take this thing and go to another place that has a better reputation, you min-max. Just swap your job for a slightly better one.

When I got out of games, I tried doing a non-games business. I tried doing the freelance stuff. I tried pretty much everything, and I was just at a complete loss on what to do next. I mean at this point, I was thinking, I don't want to stay in New York forever, and I didn't want to move for games, but I wanted to do something else.

I was really sick of the whole job application process too, because it was like, especially if you're not extremely technical and your experiences are not in programming, you weren't exactly in high demand. I wanted to invert that. I wanted it to be where I was going to be in demand and there were a lot of jobs, and so that's one of the things that drew me to doing web development because that's just what it is right now. Now, if I get fired from the company, I don't have to move to California or Texas or something. There'll be other things available right here where I am.

MW: Yeah. You know, it's interesting, the remote boom that's happening right now. A lot of the people I've spoken to have had some kind of remote gig in the interim between moving from traditional development to whatever they're doing now. Um, even I'm doing remote work as we speak. So I think that's been a really interesting thing that's kind of allowed people to get away from the big city centers because what's interesting is, I mean if you can make San Francisco money in Biloxi, Mississippi, I mean, you're living large, right?

It's definitely compelling. There's something so bizarre for me. When I was working in California, I was paid quite well. Games industry well, but quite well. And you know, you're broke. Between the cost of your commute, the cost of your vehicle, and your taxes and fees are through the roof. The housing is astronomical ... just beyond reality. The cost of every amenity is hiked way up. I mean, a bottle of beer is like $8. Most places, like, you're just, it crushes you. Every little thing is staged to financially grind you to dust.

I mean, by the time the end of the month rolls around, you have this big monster paycheck that comes in and then gets directly sent right back out the door. My wife and I saved absolutely nothing over the course of being there, which is so bizarre to me because before I moved to California ... and I was an academic beforehand, you know, I made a fraction of what I made there, but I was able to save, afford things. Do things.

The vacations and travel and all of that got the kibosh. Some of that is not the games industry's fault. Some of that's housing's fault, right? I mean the area around LA, San Francisco, the Bay Area ... it's just a super-hard place to live in for that reason. But of course you could have been in games or manufacturing or beer or whatever and that would have applied.

OK—These last two are pretty open ended. You can take them or leave them. Any words for folks who might be where you were before—minus the car crash—that you think would be good for them to hear?

BS: You mean people that are having a rough time and they're not too sure what to do?

MW: Yep, just people who are unsatisfied with where they are. Probably the kind of person that would pick up a book called "Breaking Out of the Games Industry." The kinds of things that you think they might want or need to hear. What you would tell yourself prior to your accident? That sort of thing.

BS: OK. So first thing is, it is certainly fine to think these thoughts and to explore options.

The second thing is—and this was huge for me—your identity is not tied to you working in game development. That was huge because I thought ... I make games ... I love video games. Always played them. I'd always wanted to work in games, and if I've got this thing that I always wanted ... and then I didn't want it anymore, did that make me a fraud?

If I left, would my friends in game development not be my friends anymore? A lot of it for me was identity. If I'm not a game developer, what am I? But there's a lot more to anybody's identity than what they do for a living, even if that is making games.

I guess the other thing is to figure out exactly what about the situation isn't working. Is it the hours and the working conditions? Is it that it's not scratching the itch for why you even started doing this to begin with? Is it because of instability or moving or longer-term career prospects if there's something else that you want to do, but you've been putting it off?

MW: OK, last one, wildcard question, literally anything else you'd like to add that you think ought to be in print?

BS: I was just thinking about this, I don't know if this is what you're looking for or not … but after I had done the web development program and I got my first job, I wanted to write a book, which I did, about how to get into the games industry because I had a backlog of emails from people saying things like "How can I get into games?" or "My cousin wants to get into games." … So, I would ask for some more information about them and then write an email about what that person could do next. But I started thinking, instead of doing one-off emails, it would be better to put everything down into a book because then I could just say: here is the sum total of everything I know about this, because I know a lot about breaking into games because I was, you know, doing it a couple times over 10 years and working with other people who were doing the same thing.

But I think it was important because I was out at that point. I started working on web stuff, but it was important to me to kind of store all of the stuff that I knew. I didn't want all this knowledge about how to get into games and the networking business to just evaporate because it seemed like a waste.

So on one hand, it's partly preserving some of that knowledge, and some of it will get outdated, but I think a lot of the fundamental things will stay relevant. I wanted to put that all in one place so it could help other people. And the second part was for me, because I think it was like a "closure" project. It was sort of like literally closing the book on my journey to get into games because I realized I'd gotten into it. Now I don't want to get into it anymore, or don't "need" to get into it. And just doing that as a project and finishing it felt pretty good.

So I don't know if someone else is thinking about getting out or how it's gonna look … but if they eventually do and they still feel bad or something, maybe think of some kind of a closure project. Maybe it's a small game. Maybe it's a book that can help someone.

MW: Okay, great! Thank you so much. I'm going to hit the stop button—

Clearly, Ben's story is not everyone's. Obviously, very few of us have had such harrowing near-death experiences that made it pretty obvious that we needed to get out of games before it killed us. On the other hand, many of the themes that Ben addressed in the interview regularly recur in conversations about games. Things like crunch, working out of your own time zone, long commutes, and deplorable working conditions. Thankfully, the type of work I do is relatively crunch free as far as the games industry goes, but he also discussed moving farther and farther away from actually making games, a complaint that I certainly understand.

These issues are not unique to games, but certainly, it seems that even as the games industry makes leaps and bounds toward new technologies and new ways to play and makes creative strides, we still have some very basic cleaning-up to do in terms of how we treat our employees. As I write this, Twitter is awash with stories of hundred-hour work weeks, and the games industry is in the middle of another seemingly monthly controversy about its basic compliance with labor laws, overtime, and basic human dignity.

Ish Vicens, formerly Volition

I worked with Ismael ("Ish") at Volition for a while. He was tasked with keeping our group of misfits on task, and acted as our project manager. The "release group," as it was called, was an amalgam of engineers, testers, data scientists (me), and the user research team. Thankfully, at least in my experience, this group tended to see less crunch than the rest of the development team. Although, immediately postlaunch, such groups tend to get very busy.

Ish eventually left Volition to go indie, and now works for Gun Media, the folks behind the brilliant asymmetrical competitive game *Friday the 13th: The Game.* Ish has a positive outlook on the industry, despite his leaving AAA being part of a recurring games industry trend: postproject layoffs. I hope you'll find his continued vim for the games industry through his transition to a more independent role inspiring.

MW: Hey, Ish, thanks for taking this interview. Question one, please introduce yourself the way you'd like to be referred to!

IV: Generally Ish, but ... my professional name, my full name, is Ismael Vicens, and uh, you have the spelling of that?

MW: Yep, sure do. So, what do you do now? Job title?

IV: Oh, well, still a producer. I'm a senior producer, but now it's at a small little indie. It's kind of ... I'd say "game idea group" called Gun Media.

MW: Okay. These are the guys that did *Friday the 13th*, is that right?

IV: Yeah, I mean the company essentially is a few designers and a few producers, and with *Friday*, essentially Gun came up with the idea and the core of the design, but outsourced all the development to a company in Colorado, a larger group called Illfonic that previously worked on, oh, that monster multiplayer game where one player was the monster and the others were all these hunters ...

MW: *Evolve!*

IV: Yes, that's it. Yes. They had worked on *Evolve*. So obviously, they had asymmetric multiplayer experience, which is one of the reasons that they were chosen. Same thing with Gun's first title, which was a mobile military turn-based tactical game called *Breach & Clear.* Gun came up with the ideas and of course the funding for it, and some of the design, but actual implementation and development was handled by a studio called Mighty Rabbit Studios. As for our future projects, we've got two that we're working on that are going in the same direction. We come up with ideas, write up some design docs, figure out marketing and everything like that and put together the money. But we generally don't do any development in house. Oh another project, we're functioning purely as a publisher for it, I mean we're of course involved as far as like doing marketing and trying to provide feedback and everything. But uh, we're mostly just money for this group and that's for Bloober Team, the company that did *Layers of Fear.*

MW: Okay. That's actually super cool. I go to Lexington frequently— great city, love the bourbon. So next question: I'm going to ask you a few questions about your life in games. You can anonymize or omit anything you're uncomfortable sharing or anything that's covered in an NDA or other agreement. Also, you can feel free to plug anything you are currently working on or that you will be working on by the time this gets published.

Okay. So the first question: how long have you been working in games and could you give us like a little career rundown, like how you got into this whole thing?

IV: I've been working in games for 14 years now. As far as for how I got into it, essentially I was living in Champaign, Illinois, and I randomly found out there was a video game company there. I had no idea. At that time, I was selling computers for Dell, and then I was working for an accountant so, you know, just like general early 20s to mid-20s malaise of just hopping from job to job with, uh, not exactly any real vision of what I wanted to do.

I saw an advertisement searching for QA testers, and this was when Volition was ramping up for tests on their *Punisher* title. So of course I applied and interviewed with the QA lead, and then I got hired and basically from there, man, I just realized holy shit, I love video games. I have for my whole life.

Then I started thinking, working here is amazing. And working with these people is awesome. This is a great job and I'm learning so much, I'm having a ball and making friends. So man, I just, I threw myself into it as hard as I could and when it came time to ramp down [lay off] the QA staff after the title shipped, you know, it went from like

20 people down to 5 and uh, I was one of the ones kept on, so that was awesome. And then I was one of the people that was in place to help build the QA team for *Saints Row*, which was going to be Volition's first open world title. And then over the course of that project, I ended up becoming the QA lead.

I built up the QA team bit by bit and ... that was a hard time. I trace my current hair loss and graying to being QA lead on *Saints Row*. You know, like the president when they get elected, they immediately just curdle. That is what my first real cycle in a stressful position at a gaming company did to me.

The final crunch and delivery of that title was nuts. I had pitch-black hair and then we shipped *Saints Row* and suddenly got like a salt-and-pepper beard. I'm like, "Well, fuck." But you know what it was, it was a learning experience, and it's funny, you know, when you get a lot of kids now that ask you, or just say, "I'd love to be in the game industry" ... and I'll tell them ... I am always completely honest when I say it's a great industry, get in it for one cycle and you'll know if you actually want to stay in there. It certainly has an equalizing property toward the end of production for sure. It totally does. You know, I mean it's when the shine comes off a little bit.

But, you know, but for me, the reason people do it, for me anyway, it's not because I just loved working in games. I mean, that's certainly part of it, but it's because generally the people in the industry, like the developers, the peers you're working with, not necessarily always management or c-level people, but your peers, the devs you're working with, the production people you're working with, they're just, they're awesome people. ... And so you just like to work with them, and there's very few jobs where you can work with an entire company made up of individuals who are more or less compatible. So that's the reason to stay in it.

Once *Saints Row* was starting to wrap up, Volition knew they needed some production assistance on new projects, so I applied and became an assistant producer for Red Faction Guerilla and that's where I really learned a lot. I ran design groups. Uh, I ran localization, a lot of outsourcing. I also managed some of the DLC as well as the PC port of the project and so it was just like, right away, I completely dove into production land and I loved it. So from there, it just evolved through going to *Saints Row: The Third* where I did more of that at a higher level, you know, responsible for bigger areas and projects with larger portions of the budget, for instance.

Then I moved on to *Zeus*, the canceled original IP at Volition, which … it totally can be talked about because I believe [Greg] Donovan presented about it at GDC. I worked on *Zeus* for a long time and then eventually once we were acquired by Deep Silver it turned into project management. So just steadily working through production, working on bigger areas. Bigger and bigger areas until finally I was in that "release group," which was just using my skills from production but was generally more technically oriented, and this was just happenstance just because of the way projects will ramp up and ramp down. I always ended up being the last person on a project, you know, the guy that turned out the lights and so they just decided that the "release group" that they were forming up suited my experience. It wasn't necessarily my dream to work in that group, but it made sense and it was the best thing for the studio at that time.

MW: Thank you. The next one is a little bit more humanizing and if you have a squishy anecdote, that's great. If not, that's fine too. But the next question is, "Describe when you first knew you wanted to work in video games." I think you kinda covered this a little bit with your transition from a more traditional job into games, but if you had like a bit of an epiphany moment about how wonderful it actually is to work in games, like the good side, I would love to hear that.

IV: For me, it was right away going into QA. At first, it was a little intimidating and so I would say when we were getting towards the tail end of testing even on that first project, um, two things happened. First, because the build was relatively stable, [our team] were the first to run a version of the game and beat critical path. And immediately, my boss was like, that is awesome. And it happened to fall on the day that *Halo 2* released. So he handed me 50 bucks and was like, go to Best Buy and buy me a copy of *Halo 2*. That's awesome. Up to then, I hadn't had jobs where there was that camaraderie and that looseness and that like, you know, sense of fun.

Everything I'd had previously was just, like I said, standard young person job, which generally is a bit more rote and a bit more structured and kind of grinding and boring.

... and then the other was um, we were preparing our one of our trailers and a demo and we were trying to get a Guinness World Record for being the game with the most ways to kill someone. A company email got sent out for people to play the demo and try to spotlight how many ways we could murder an NPC. This is a companywide email. Awesome. We're trying to get the record for the video game with the most ways to kill people. So I had to sit there and carefully note in an Excel file every single way I could kill someone in the game.

It was things like that back and forth in a very short window that made me think ... "there's never going to be another job like this." I guess unless I like go work at like a movie company or something, which I know nothing about. And video games I know. So obviously I need to stay here.

MW: Okay. So the question that I usually follow up with is, "How did you get your start in the games industry?" Um, but you've kind of already hit that. So let me skip to the next one. "What made you make the jump from a traditional games role?" Like working at a traditional AAA-type to kind of a more nontraditional studio: the sort of thing that you're in now.

IV: Well, I mean with Volition, there were some pretty big layoffs, you know, so the layoffs occurred and I was caught up in them. I immediately started applying to multiple studios and I mean, and I'm not trying to sound arrogant or anything, but every studio I applied to, I interviewed and was offered a position, but my wife and I quickly realized, you know, she's from Champaign, which is a smaller area, and I just knew that I didn't think city living was the kind of atmosphere that either of us wanted.

We're people that at this point ... we enjoy our space. We like taking our dogs out, we like having a big Halloween display ... Just these kinds of things that made me realize I don't want to live in a big city, you know. And that of course starts to significantly narrow the field with video game companies. So immediately I've got to strike, probably like 60%, 70% at least, of the game studios that are out there ...

at least in the States. And then next after that, there were some places that were still relatively well suited, but I realized several of them were basically ... I would say continuing my career as opposed to changing and potentially enhancing or moving my career.

I could have gone to work at a company where I would have just done stuff I was already doing at Volition and just continued in that, stayed comfortable, made a good living and, and know "Okay I'm, I'm comfortable with this job, I can do this job and I get to keep working in games." But, you know, the opportunity here at Gun came up and there was one other opportunity that also I would say was similarly disruptive in altering the trajectory of my career to some degree. And it was between them and here at Gun.... And to be frank, I chose Gun for a couple of reasons. One, I like Lexington better than the location with the other company. And then Gun, you know, they did *Friday the 13th* and they're all horror fans. How could I say no? With my background?

MW: Haha, sure, I get it. So, next I typically ask people if there was a breaking point or red flag, something that made you say to yourself: "I'm not going to do this anymore." In your case, I think that's the layoffs, right?

IV: You know, I mean despite the layoffs, and this isn't to speak ill of the company, but I think there was some amount of Stockholm Syndrome there. It eventually becomes such that staying with something is easy because it's there, you're used to it and you don't see the daily potential slipping of some of your love for something.

MW: Like the sunk cost fallacy. Where do you spend a long time doing something and you're like, well, I'm 10 years in. I don't want to change.

IV: Exactly. But it's not even that ... sometimes people just completely have blinders to red flags that are happening. I mean, I'm not gonna say that if the layoff hadn't happened, I wouldn't still be there. But I'd like to think that like at some point, maybe within that time frame, maybe a little later, I would hope that my eyes started to go wide and then say, you know what? Maybe it's time to move on. And, you know, I mean with gaming companies, generally people move on within a very short time period for different reasons. A lot of it is they just want to studio-hop until they either end up somewhere they love or end up in a more senior position. My move from Volition wasn't like that. But, you know, I think I've done a lot of time there. So maybe it was time.

MW: Before the layoffs actually happened at Volition, there were a lot of people jumping ship. There was a period of time there about a year leading in where people were going every other week. I think people kind of sense when something ugly is coming … that's certainly been my experience at other studios as well.

IV: I would say that that's definitely true. A lot of people that left were people that had been around the industry. I think they "got it" more than some of the Volition lifers, because that's not something that they had experienced before. Whereas those people who had been around the industry had experienced it and I think they were able to see the signs. It's like an animal's sense of a coming earthquake type of thing.

MW: Yeah. I mean there's something, I don't know exactly what it is to this day, but I mean it's happened, like there were layoffs at PlayStation while I was there. I've seen this more than once.

We went to a "layoff lunch"—and I'm sad that there's a word for this—a whole bunch of people were laid off and run out of our studio at PlayStation—security escorts, that kind of thing—and everyone who isn't laid off kind of just goes away for the day to let those people kinda deal with it.

IV: Yeah.

MW: So you sort of go have lunch, whatever, the company pays to get you out of the way for the day and make things less awkward for everyone watching their friends get fired.

And I was sitting having lunch with like a half-dozen people. And every one of them was like, were sort of—how do we deal with this?—and every single person at the table was like—oh, this isn't my first layoff lunch; this is nothing—[laughs] As though it's just this thing that just happens. Kind of an odd sort of thing. A lot of crying, a lot of people wondering about their kids. Really tough to deal with.

IV: And to be honest, I keep in touch with a bunch of people at Volition; I'm sure you do as well.

MW: Oh yeah.

IV: I don't think necessarily that trend that you've were speaking of has … It hasn't abated that much; there still seems to be at least to some degree a general exodus. And part of that could just be that once that layoff happened, again, that was not something that had happened with Volition before; it might have fundamentally altered the atmosphere or the character of that company to some people, I'm not sure. But that can definitely happen.

MW: And, if I read correctly, they got reacquired by a company that's kind of THQ again?

IV: They got reacquired by a company that had acquired a bunch of the random stuff leftover from the death of THQ.

MW: It was like, Nordic Games. Right?

IV: Yeah. Exactly.

MW: How bizarre is that?

IV: I know.

MW: It's done a full circle back to THQ, sort of.

IV: Yeah. THQ just … Not in California this time. I don't remember where. They're somewhere in … somewhere in Europe as well.

MW: So, this is another emotional question.

When we talk about animals sensing an earthquake, that kind of thing where you're thinking, "Ah, I better start looking for other jobs," what do you think at the core is missing from what you're doing that makes a person, kind of look around? Like why are you looking for something other, what was it that made you kind of be like, "Maybe it's time, maybe it's time to make a switch."

IV: I think, at least from my perspective at Volition, and looking back on it now, having the ability to reflect on my last several months to a year there, I think part of it was … It just could have been because we were all so "heads down" trying to close out the project. But people just get very secure and specialized in their roles, and it's almost like we became more rigid. And part of that is, you want to be a little more conservative when you're finally trying to get something out the door. You want to take less risk.

MW: Sure.

IV: But it just felt like, as a company, there was less of an ability for the company to try and exercise some kind of creative control over what they really wanted to do. And from an individual standpoint, it also meant that we were kind of starting to feel a little stuck in our roles, with little ability to effect change.

And part of that was also just because the publisher was generally trying to impose more of their structure, as opposed to previously at Volition [where] we'd had a lot of latitude I think to kind of do things that we wanted to do as long as delivery occurred, or as long as the information that we passed along satisfied the real request or the real needs of the publisher.

Whereas with the current publisher it was more like—it may satisfy it, but we want you to actually also just deliver it the way we want to deliver it—and things like that.

It started to feel a little more, like I said, less … I don't know. "Fun" is not the right word, right?

MW: In user research, we often jokingly say "fun" is a buzzword. Because it's hard to quantify what that actually means.

But yeah, I get what you mean. You're certainly not the first person, and I doubt you'll be the last person, to articulate that there is a friction between the publisher and the actual developer in a third-party development relationship. I think that's been echoed a few times and certainly I'm sure I'll hear it again.

IV: The thing is, though, and I do want to make it clear, I don't feel that there was necessarily friction between the individuals. It's really hard to quantify. Because every individual I worked with at the publisher level—well, OK—most of the individuals I worked with at publisher level were wonderful people, and a lot of times, maybe this was also just due to cultural differences because obviously our publisher at that time was located in Germany; we were in the Midwest United States. Once we'd actually established a common vocabulary and a common understanding of the intent behind things on both sides, established what we were trying to get across to one another, generally communication became a lot more streamlined, easy. And I made a lot of friends with people at our publisher there as well.

It's more like the institution of it, the bureaucracy of it, once it starts to aggregate into all these separate pieces and each individual piece is actually a great person to work with who seems to be asking something totally reasonable, but once they start to create this bureaucracy of all these different asks ... and I think it had to do with specifically how that was structured, which was not a very hierarchical structure with clear reporting lines—that's what made it difficult there.

So the people were great, but I think that organization in particular was not structured in a way that made it easy to work with once you put it all together. And of course from a production standpoint, you're generally dealing with a wider variety of people than anyone else. So that's where it became difficult, right, because suddenly you're ...

Like with THQ, for example, we dealt with a couple people at the publisher and then all that information was funneled through them to the wider structure of THQ, with Deep Silver, I think this was a growing pain. When they bought us, we were like their first major development studio and then suddenly they snapped up several more—they hadn't yet adopted a structure that allowed for us to funnel information like that. So instead you get multiple groups coming at you at the same time, and that overhead just became so onerous. And that was the problem. So never the individuals. Like I said, the individuals I work with generally were awesome people.

MW: Yeah.

OK. I generally shift into logistics here. So one of the things we're trying to address with people for sort of the target audience of the book is that you need to untie your identity as a professional from games.

So, you are a valuable person outside of games. One of the things I hear a lot of the time is—if I don't work in games anymore, who am I? You know? I'm used to being that guy that works in games—there's this kind of identity piece to it.

So one of the things that I've been trying to address with my conversations with friends and with this book is that people shouldn't be afraid to seek new opportunities whenever. So we typically ask, how did you do it? How did you ...

But in your case, I don't think you had too much of a choice. [laughs]

IV: Exactly.

MW: For example, I often ask, "How did you mull up the sort of chutzpah to go in and quit?" But, I suppose, well, you didn't really have a whole lot of choice in the matter.

So I'm going to skip that, and I'm going to ask you to describe a little bit more about what you do now, in terms of what your day to day looks like as compared to working in a more traditional AAA role.

IV: It is surprisingly different in so many ways. In a AAA role, I would say there's so much institutional knowledge built up over the course of multiple titles across potentially multiple studios with so much reference and people you can ask, and blah, blah, blah.

At Volition, a big part of being a producer is not necessarily knowing the answers but knowing who will have the answers and kind of being a focal point for collection of that information, and then passing that information, and you know, funneling it, and putting it in the right direction.

We're basically like the creepy vacuum tube system of mail, like those old-built skyscrapers. We're in the mail room.

Now at Gun, holy crap, it's so different. In a single day I could be working on a marketing plan while touching up language in a contract with IP holders while looking at the QA results from a patch we want to apply to the game we currently have out, while also touching up a design doc. Because at Gun, we're so small, everyone's involved in everything. You know?

MW: It sounds a bit like a startup.

IV: Yeah.

And you know, I think we kind of want to stay that size and make sure that we're all invested in what we're doing so that we're never too specialized. Like, sure, there's some knowledge I brought to the table working at Gun; I'm helping to work through some of the things like figuring out how to better schedule some of the projects that they're working on, figuring out how better to speak "game" ... Almost no one that worked at Gun had come from games at all. It was all people who came from outside of development. So they had no idea. So I'm helping them to translate, OK, so when our developer says this, here's really what's going on and what the impact is for the project. They don't speak that language.

But my day to day is so much more varied and so much more hands-on with a lot of areas I never would have been hands-on before: it's awesome, you know, it's a totally different day to day. I can't predict my days nearly as well as I could at Volition. But I think that's great. It gives me a lot more stuff to work on. It also just means that I'm much more invested in working with my coworkers and communicating with them all the time. And that means face to face in person. It's a small company, and that makes it good, too.

Like even at Volition—stupid, right?—but you work at a 200-person studio and then someone's just down the hall, but you still Skype them or still send them an email.

MW: Yep.

IV: You get to that creepy point. Right?

Whereas at Gun, basically I am getting up and talking to people all the time.

MW: Do you think there's a magic number for a studio?

IV: I don't. I don't know. I haven't had enough experience across a variety of studios to really be able to know that.

MW: Sure.

IV: I would say that people who have been with a studio that's grown probably would be able to tell you that better. I know from experience talking to some other people, most of them would say that they would guess 50 people is about the upper bounds of really what they want. And I think part of that is because

50 people still seems like a manageable amount to where you can maybe just get by with one person doing all the planning and everyone else knowing each other. You know?

MW: Interesting. Yeah, a few people have talked about this. One of the things I've had articulated at a few of these interviews is that people left AAA to go to a more indie role because they just wanted to be more involved in things.

It's a really common sentiment—I left Triple-A because—and the fill-in-the-blank is, say it was an animator, for example—I got to a point where instead of being the guy who does all the characters, I was the guy who did all of the hubcaps, like it got so unbelievably specialized.

IV: That's how Disney got where they were like, this one dude does like cloud outlines.

I mean, I understand that, that kind of ... And I'm sure Ubisoft with, like, 30,000 individuals totally works like that. I totally get that from an efficiency standpoint. But when you're talking about a creative industry, there is something inherently stifling about that.

So maybe, I don't know, maybe the whole process of—there was actually an article not too long ago that was about a lot of Japanese studios that are very much like what Gun is, which is a small creative group that's then contracting out the development, and maybe that kind of smaller separation where it's a couple of different groups coming together to make a game as opposed to like a large monolithic group—maybe that's more favored towards a developer who wants to feel a bigger sense of contribution.

MW: You would not be the first person that's said that to me ... that we're moving toward a place where it's like maybe there are a few creative people that kind of outsource. And it's interesting, I didn't actually know Gun was structured that way. So I'm learning as I do these.

IV: I think it totally makes sense. And I think the corollaries to the film industry do hold up to some degree in that, even working at Volition, I met a bunch of people who kind of just wanted to get in, do their piece, and get out, like a contractor.

MW: Right.

IV: Like, they never engage with the full vision of the project unless they were forced to.

MW: Right. I mean, that's certainly true for like voice talents and things. You know what I mean. For Christ's sake, we had Sasha Grey kicking around [at Volition for *Saints Row: The Third*].

IV: Well, why do you need a programmer? Half our programmers never played the game except to potentially reproduce a bug. And even then, half the time, they would just have a QA person come to their desk and do it.

One of the employees at Volition made a point of letting us know he'd never played one of our games until he was made a lead on *Agents of Mayhem*. He said he made a point to never play our games until they're on store shelves and he's like—I don't want to play an in-development buggy game. He's like, I just want to model the vehicle they told me to and go home.

MW: It's interesting. I don't think there's anything necessarily bad about that. I think we're just having a bit of a collision between the people that wanted to be Hideo Kojima, and have a complete kind of auteur level of control over everything, and the reality of a growing industry, which is one where eventually you're going to have people in there that want to come in at 9:00 AM and they want to work on some fucking tree textures and then they want to go the fuck home and not touch it at all in between. These are totally different, but equally important, people.

IV: Again, it's not necessarily a bad thing. Tools to some degree will become more standardized and efficient. So, like, look at the explosion of indie filmmakers, short filmmakers, Internet filmmakers, once digital cameras and nonlinear editing on a PC or Mac or whatever became so simple. Right? So suddenly someone who just spent a little bit of money and had some good amount of knowledge and vision could create something that, at least from a visual standpoint, could rival anything you're going to see in a theater. Right?

And I think gaming could potentially have that. Once the tools and the accepted vocabulary of game designing, game UX, and everything like that become a little more flattened—and we're talking years from now, right? Like that stuff is still all fucking experimental as all hell. Even with a robust indie game studio.

But once that stuff becomes flattened a little bit, I think you'll see, you don't necessarily need just the small creative group and then like a billion people making assets. Instead, some of that stuff will simply be available for others to use and start going in and noodling around. With people who have a little bit of vision, maybe a little bit of talent.

MW: Yeah, I agree.

Back to the logistics for a second. One of the questions that other people have had and that I'm trying to address here is this how-do-you-do-it question for people that are trying to leave. And I think one of the things that sticks in their minds is the financials. So I'm going to ask you some questions about that, and you can perfectly tell me to fuck myself if they're too personal or invasive or anything.

IV: Sure.

MW: Yeah. So one of the fears with layoffs that people have is that their financial situation will precipitously decline. So there are people who stay in a job—to give you kind of the hypothetical—that are in a job and they're staying in the job because they feel like the layoff is easier to deal with, because layoffs in the games industry are quite visible, rather than just quitting and trying to find something new. So they're almost waiting for the ax man to come so that they can be visibly laid off and quickly find work at another studio.

What I want to elucidate is, did you take a really hard financial hit—if you are comfortable sharing that—when you left and when you were laid off? Or did you have a relatively quick turnover? Did you feel like it was a really hard time?

IV: Of course it was frightening. But since I moved so quickly towards interviews and job offers, there was essentially no actual bad time for us. And I'd say we probably ended up a little cash positive overall, just, the offers I received were all better.

MW: Oh wow. That's. Not common.

IV: I was doing significantly better. And with sign-on bonuses that were larger than I'd expected or even anticipated receiving. I think we ended up cash positive.

MW: That's awesome. Honestly, when I'd heard …

IV: Yeah, it was probably good for us. [laughs]

MW: When I had heard that the layoffs had touched you and some other folks, I was quite worried, like anyone would be. But I'm happy to hear that.

  Then the follow-up question is … did you have to use savings and run a second job in the interim to make sure you could get the new venture off the ground? But I mean, obviously for you, the answer is no. [laughs] So I guess I will move on.

IV: Yeah.

MW: So you've kind of already touched on this, but these questions are more about your new role. You've kind of touched on it a bit already, but there's worries in AAA that people are quite used to—Are we going to meet this deadline? Is this going to pass a particular milestone? Are we going to run over budget?—now that you're working in a more "nontraditional" space, this is kind of a new thing, what are your daily struggles, daily worries as compared to when you were in AAA?

IV: One of the big daily worries for me, since I'm not hands on with the development, is, "Will I be able to get clear and usable information from our development partner that actually will give me a good idea as to the status of a project at any given time?"

  Because I've worked on the other end of those communications—like, now, from a publisher perspective, sometimes I'm asking hard questions and being a bit of a dick to our development partner. And it's not that I want to be a dick, but now suddenly I see why our publisher, when I worked with Volition, asked us questions the way they did, and were sometimes a little aggressive.

  It's because you're not there. You can't just go down the hallway and say, hey, how's that bug going?

MW: Yeah.

IV: You've got to talk to a couple point people, hope they have the information right, and then kind of cross your fingers. Right? And that's worrying to me. The state of the project we're working on at Volition was always something that I always felt like I'd get a very clear answer within an hour of it popping in my head to go find out.

Now it's like there's maybe days of turnaround before I really can get anything approaching even a part of that clarity that I had at Volition. So, it's worrying, right? Because, like, I never feel like I've got quite as much of a handle.

MW: Yeah. And I can certainly understand that having things out of house would stress you out a little bit.

IV: Totally. And I'd say right now that's one of my big ones.

And another is, of course, since we're a publisher ... It's funny when we talk about layoffs being scary, but, I mean, at the other side of that from a publisher perspective, well, I mean, there is no entity behind you that may say, OK, this project didn't do well, but we can absorb it and keep going, where you just sweat for a minute to see if they are going to lay you off. With this, it's more like ... We need to make that money back, because you don't have someone standing there to pat us on the head and be like, it's OK this time.

MW: Yeah, exactly. Well, all right. Yeah, I guess that's kind of harrowing. Sort of an interesting thing. It feels a bit like you're talking about a role that's a touch more entrepreneurial than I think you get in AAA.

IV: Yeah.

MW: So I think that kind of flows into the next question. I typically ask people how it's different from your time in mainstream, but I think that touches on that quite nicely. What are some of the positives now? What do you like better now about working in this more flexible environment than you did about your AAA day to day?

IV: I like the fact that instead of everyone feeling like they they've got a specific role, I feel like everyone at the company I'm working on right now is heavily invested and involved in the projects. Like ideas can come from anywhere, and that's not just lip service. Now it actually really means, like, seriously, ideas can come from anywhere and we'll all discuss them and be like, hey, let's do that, that's awesome.

It's a lot less stratified as far as like, OK, over here are the people that really make these design decisions and you just do the schedule.

MW: Yeah.

IV: Not like, we will tell you you have input, and sometimes we listen to you. Instead now, it's like, no, really, we're taking this into our own hands.

That speaks to why I chose this company as the one to accept the offer. The projects that I'm actually getting to work on are near and dear to my heart. And I can't say what they are yet, only to say that again, you know me as a horror fan. You can tell that getting to work at a company that obviously is going to specialize in horror to some degree, that's very special to me. So that's something that's really awesome. Like, I've always just wanted to put passion and care into the projects I was working on, because I wanted to do a good job with them and I believed in my coworkers. But now I'm like—fuck yes, I believe in this project because it's awesome.

MW: I get it. I get it. For sure. And I think that's really important. It's not just believing in the people you work with, but what you actually do. And so I think that's a nice confluence of things.

I go into this—"Do you think it's a good decision overall?" And obviously you'll say yes. But the next question is a little more philosophical, and it is: If you hadn't had your layoff or a nasty event that made you leave, do you think if you knew this job was available as it is, you would have taken it over your AAA job?

IV: You know, at the very least, probably something I would've considered and had to have a hard conversation with my wife about.

To be honest, I was so comfortable in my AAA job, as you put it, that I wasn't even—

MW: Well, it's sort of AAA, AA, whatever you want to call Volition. But you know...

IV: Yeah. Maybe A. Or BBB.

MW: [laughs] I like BBB a lot.
Carry on. Sorry.

IV: I will say I wasn't paying attention to other jobs. And generally because of just how you think of the industry, when I did think of—oh, if I ever leave Volition—it was always about moving to another AAA studio because the idea of indie never even crossed my mind. And the idea that another weird island, like Champaign, like Volition in Champaign, that an island of Gun in Lexington could exist was never even in my brain at all. I was just comparing apples to apples. I wasn't even looking for whatever the hell you would call what I have now.

MW: You know, to wax philosophical for a minute. I think, and if I had to put money on this, I think the games industry is in a place where the American beer industry was about 20 years ago—if you told somebody in 1995 or so that you really liked American beer, they'd be pretty likely to laugh at you. Right? Because there were really like three brands of beer that were essentially competing for the same market, and they weren't really doing anything too interesting. If you looked at games in the '90s, it was like Sega versus Nintendo with a few fringe things. Indies were nonexistent after the '83 crash, and it was all platform controlled and publisher controlled. Very little decentralization. If Bill and Jim wanted to make a game in their basement, that was basically impossible save for some kind of hacky workarounds.

So the access and the decentralization has skyrocketed. If you and I wanted to fuck around on Skype, we can put together a platformer like tomorrow in Unity or in Construct or in something easy and accessible. And given the knowledge of the industry, we might even do half decently, you know?

So I think that decentralization is causing people to kind of reevaluate—all right, I pay $5,000 a month for my Bay-Area, 400-square-foot apartment. Like, maybe I can do this myself in a place that is an island, as you put it, in a Lexington or a Champaign or an Erie, Pennsylvania, or in any of these places.

So, in fairness, I think you're going to see more and more of these. And I think that can only help the country economically. So I'm happy to hear that you found a place that's kind of smaller.

OK, the last two are total wild cards. This is it. This one is, when you were in that spot at Volition, kind of comfortable and complacent in the job, but sort of with a few of those lingering concerns, thinking maybe it's time for a change, do you have some words for "past" Ish that you think "now" Ish would say to him that he needed to hear at the time? Because I'm trying to speak directly to individuals that are in that space that might benefit from some of the kinds of thoughts you have now in hindsight.

IV: That's a really good question. I would say that's ...

Even though it's important to want to do what's best for the studio, at the same time, you still have to think about what's best for you. And that doesn't just mean trying to keep your career safe. It means, what is actually going to help your career? And when that means doing something that's uncomfortable, either at the job you're at now or potentially thinking about leaving that job so that you can expand what you're doing—you have to potentially make that leap. Like, don't get stuck in a rut, essentially. And just think, oh man, I'm becoming more skilled at this specific area.

Like we've been talking about, game development is still such a young industry with so many different potential ways to approach it. I don't think it's useful at this point to become so specialized in a specific area unless you have no interest in doing anything else. Like unless you're the guy that does just want to say I'm the rivet modeler, and you're comfortable with that, don't let yourself self-select becoming super specialized. Fuck that. Go do something exciting and different and crazy.

MW: I like that. It's come up. Exactly as you put it, it's come up. Between you and others who've made a good change out of a relatively negative situation. Other people I've interviewed from the gamut of "left on completely amicable terms to just seek a different career," to "left on completely not amicable terms, to get the hell out"—every single one of you, as a common thread, has said, I'm so glad I changed because now

I can effect creative change. It's been a common thread with absolutely everybody.

So I think that runs in our blood as developers to some extent. I don't think anybody who really cares about beer wants to work at Budweiser and just shovel mash into a tun all day.

IV: [laughs]

MW: I don't think they want to … like, to specify that one role, to be the guy who checks the yeast proliferation in Tank C … it's just too limiting for people.

So it's interesting. I don't know how the industry moves forward from that. But it's been really interesting to hear people's different perspectives on it.

IV: Well, I guess it's … first, figure out if you are the guy that wants to just check Tank C, and if you are, and you're comfortable doing that, fucking do that as best you can, man. And be happy about that. You know?

MW: Exactly. Because on the other hand, and I haven't spoken to any of them yet, but there definitely are people—I mean, for this book; I've certainly spoken to a ton in my career—there are definitely people who were like, "I am the best combat model rigger that exists."

IV: Exactly. And that's awesome.

MW: There's definitely pride in being the guy or girl who is phenomenal at that particular job. I feel like the people who make the jump to indie stuff have a bit of the entrepreneurial spark. I feel like they'd want to get away for the purpose of taking on a wider role as opposed to a deeper role.

That definitely has been a recurring theme for everything, everyone that I've spoken to.

IV: Sure.

MW: All right. Last one, easy. Wildcard—throw in anything at all you'd like to add that you would like to see in a book about people considering leaving a traditional role in the games industry. And again, no pressure. Just literally anything.

IV: I would say … man, that's tough.

MW: [laughs]

IV: Well, for anyone that's considering leaving a role in the traditional gaming industry, make sure you're not doing it for the wrong reasons, and that's not to discourage anyone from doing it. I just don't think anyone should have been ... A lot of people that get into games do it because they're passionate about it, and passionate people can feel emotions, potentially, of course, very strongly—I would never want someone leaving an industry in anger. Especially if it's something they love. Consider instead of leaving the industry, how do you take your skills and apply them in a different way? Or—decide, has your passion changed to something else? Like, has your passion said, you know what, I just need family time, and all I need is a career that supports that family time because that's my new passion.

But what, if anything, the industry has shown us, for people that are willing to enter the gaming industry, obviously you can get a job or at least make money ... at least make a living doing something you love. You can be happy at least for some time doing something you absolutely love in a field people love. So make sure that you are still satisfying some condition of your passion to make yourself happy.

I think what's really important is that, being in the game industry taught me that I don't have to just work a fucking nine to five job, you know, wearing a suit. And even if I didn't already love the game industry, I would always have to be working in a direction that still allowed me to be satisfied and happy with my life. Like, I'm not saying I wouldn't necessarily go into another creative field. Maybe I would, but if I did, it would be because there's some other part of the work satisfying whatever that new need or discovery within me is.

MW: I understand.

OK. That is it. I can press the stop button.

Layoffs. Another common theme in the games industry. When a project goes south, often the ones left holding the bag are the developers. Even if a project is successful, executives have often planned to lay off a significant chunk of the workforce immediately after shipping the product. There is a bitter irony in that.

If an executive decides that making a great *Multiplayer Online Battle Arena* is a smart decision, and 300 employees spend three years pouring their hearts and souls into that MOBA, and then at launch the MOBA ships have sailed, often the development staff are shuffled off. On the other hand, if the MOBA launches and is a smash success, the need for low-level engine programmers, animators, and new content producers is understandably diminished, and the layoffs happen anyway.

Unfortunately, no amount of preparation, hard work, or quality on the part of any one developer could have solved Ish's problem, nor the same problem for any of the other thousands of game workers who face cyclical layoffs every year.

In my own personal experience, watching games like *Agents of Mayhem* do poorly despite the fabulously talented animators, artists, writers, programmers, and more who spent an inordinate amount of time on the game, it does seem a bit unjust. Perhaps Ish's prediction that the games industry will become more contractor driven, like the film industry, is sage wisdom. In such a situation, all of the development staff are paid and move on to another game regardless of the title's performance.

Regardless, sometimes making a big career move like the one Ish made comes involuntarily. Certainly we see this in the games industry with layoff pizza parties and the like. Whether this happens in other industries I can't say, but for Ish, things are looking up.

Ed Kay, formerly Codemasters, Epic, LucasArts, and others

Ed is one of those old games industry salts. He's been in numerous studios, and eventually decided after a lengthy career that it was time to make a change. Both he and Nigel Kershaw, interviewed later in this book, fit that description. While they share different perspectives, the change has been positive for them both.

Careful readers will also note that both Ed Kay and Ben Serviss worked on *TimeShift*, though in different roles at completely different times, and in different countries. Another recurrent theme in the games industry—despite being large and profitable, the interconnectedness of the industry makes it feel very small.

MW: OK! So, number one, introduce yourself the way you would like to be introduced in the book.

EK: Yeah. So, I'm Edward Kay. And I've worked in video games about 15 years, and the past two years I've been an independent developer. I left a career in AAA working on console games to start working on my own thing.

MW: Oh, very cool. One of the things I'd like to sort of elucidate is kind of a little career rundown for you. So, like, if you could give me a very basic high level—I worked here on this, then I worked here on this. That'd be really helpful.

EK: Yeah, sure. Could take a bit of time.

MW: That's OK.

EK: Yeah, I've worked for about, I think about 10 different companies or something like that. Not necessarily because I was getting bored of a particular job or anything. It's more just a product of the games industry being so unstable, to be honest.

MW: Right. No, I understand that.

EK: I'd say almost, not every job, but most jobs that I changed, I changed because I finished a game, but it didn't sell as well as the company hoped for and then the company ran out of money. So that's definitely happened a lot.

Just to try and give you a brief summary. I did computer science at university. I've always been interested in games ever since I was younger. Obviously played tons of games as a kid, especially in the arcade, but also, Amstrad games as well. An Amstrad home computer.

MW: Yes.

EK: And then a lot of console gaming with the Sega Genesis and so on.

I never really thought that video games could be a career, I guess. I think I got my first computer probably when I was like 14 or something and I fiddled around a lot with sort of editing games. Like, I got very into *Doom* and sort of editing that, trying to build levels, failing mostly. But doing a lot of editing, of gameplay and so on, with some of the editors that were available, and I really enjoyed that kind of thing. But I never thought that that could be anything serious.

But then a university friend of mine ended up graduating a year before me because he'd done a [Bachelor of Science] and I'd done a Masters, and then he got a job at Rare. I had no idea that you could do computer science and get a job in video games. I just didn't even think that this could be possible. So then I thought, why not try and do the same? So, I graduated a year later and got a job at Codemasters as a programmer. So that was sort of my first start in the industry.

MW: OK.

EK: It sort of shuttered all my dreams a little bit. Because it has me thinking—wow, video games, this is going to be amazing, super creative, and so on—but it wasn't at all.

I was working on a football game and it was called *Club Football*. It just wasn't an interesting role for me anyway. And I was doing programming of the UI, and also with some visual effects in the game, like a system for doing special effects. And it wasn't very creative, basically. The game itself was a pretty standard football game, and the work itself was not very interesting.

I did that for about a year, but I was sort of thinking— man, I really want to get involved in design; that would be a lot more creative, a lot more interesting—but I couldn't find a way to do that at Codemasters itself on any of the other projects.

So I looked for another job and I got my first role as a designer at Head First which is—back then, that company was sort of famous for making *Simon the Sorcerer*. But they were working on a new game, which was a horror game called *Call of Cthulhu: Dark Corners of the Earth*. Have you ever heard of that game?

MW: Yeah. I haven't played it. I've heard of it though, for sure.

EK: It kind of became a bit of a cult classic. But yeah, so that was my kind of transition to design. That was as a level scripter.

Which basically meant that you would be taking levels and scripting game play into them. It was like a sort of horror adventure stealth game, I guess.

MW: I think this is a bit like "technical designer" nowadays.

EK: Yeah. Exactly.

So it still used the programming background. But it meant that I got to dip my toes into design. So it was perfect, basically.

MW: Sure.

EK: I spent probably about three years there. Most of that on *Dark Corners*. Because that game was sort of in the early stages of development when I got that. But it was a hugely ambitious game. And we were also trying to … Well, originally, it was a PC game, but then we ended up signing a deal to do it on Xbox, so that was a mountain of work and that was probably what I'd say definitely the time in my career that I've done the most crunch for sure.

MW: Sure, I can understand that.

EK: And I think that's kind of fairly typical when you're quite young—it's the first job where you're really enjoying it—and you really care about the project, care about the team.

That was an incredibly large amount of overtime myself and a bunch of people did on that project. But, fortunately we did ship. It got some mixed reviews, but it got some good ones for sure. Unfortunately, though, it didn't sell super well at the time. So it wasn't quite enough to keep the company going. And some of their other deals fell through. And that was when I experienced my first layoffs, not the most pleasant experience, you know, especially when you pour your heart into something. We probably worked overtime for something like a year. It was ridiculous.

MW: Sure.

EK: Just like a gradual—more and more hours every week kind of thing—just a little bit of extra here, like, work a couple of hours extra on this day once or twice a week. And then it just built up to four days, five days, and then the weekend. It's just, yeah, eventually it just got kind of crazy.

MW: Yeah. That's one of those insidious things where it's a little bit here and there and until you're literally always in the studio.

EK: Yeah. Yeah. And you kind of don't really notice what's happening. And then also once you're there, you've been working like a crazy amount. Well, I mean, quite a few of us got health problems. I think I had some sort of dizziness, constant headache type of thing, which I just knew was completely not normal.

MW: Right.

EK: And I just realized it was just too much, just working too much. And yeah, I needed to ease off, but that took a long time for me to kind of realize what was going on.

So that was certainly a mixture of positive and negative experiences. It was amazing working on that game, and it was definitely my first taste of actually being a designer and designing something and seeing it all the way to completion. And seeing it in the final game—that side of it was amazing and it was a super awesome team to work with, I just learned so much and had a load of fun. But very, very, very hard in terms of the overtime and so on.

MW: I can understand.

EK: Sorry, am I going into too much detail. Or do you want me to …

MW: Normally, I break this into several questions, like—describe your layoff experience—so if you just want to continue, that's perfectly fine because it's stream of consciousness and that works fine with me. Hearing about your experience is invaluable.

EK: Well whatever you prefer, if you want me to go into more detail, just let me know, or if you want me to be briefer, just let me know.

MW: That's totally fine. Yeah. I think we're up at the end of Codemasters at the moment.

EK: Ah, yes. As I said, that company did unfortunately close down because they didn't manage to secure another publishing deal.

So from then, I actually went to work for Swordfish, which was a substudio with Vivendi.

MW: OK.

EK: Vivendi had a bunch of studios, and Swordfish was their one in the UK. And that was to work on a game called *Covert One*, a game about an upcoming TV series. Unfortunately the TV series didn't do so well, the first few episodes, kind of ... Well, the first season or whatever it was, just didn't pick up very well. So that game actually got canceled after a year.

MW: Got it.

EK: But that was a technical designer role. And it was quite a shift, really, because it was a much bigger company. Head First was probably about ... The team on *Cthulhu* was maybe 15 or 20 or something. It was quite small. But Swordfish, it must have been close to 50 or something. So it was a lot bigger. And it was very different. It was definitely quite hard to adjust to that larger team structure and having a lot less creative input.

So anyway, we were working on this *Covert One* game, and, as I said, unfortunately, the series didn't do so well. So Vivendi decided not to go ahead with producing that game. And at the time, they were looking for someone to work on a 50 Cent game, so that they'd had the original, the first 50 Cent game and they were looking to make another one. And they basically decided that Swordfish were the right team for the job because they'd done a sort of a shooter before called *Cold Winter*, and then also, the *Covert One* game that we were working was almost a sort of a shooter sort of action adventure game. So we ended up starting on a *50 Cent: Blood on the Sand—*

MW: Oh, I remember seeing that.

EK: So yeah, next two years I spent working on that, basically. It was probably less than two years. It was quite a short-term development cycle really.

Yeah, did you ever play that game?

MW: I have. That one I have played on PlayStation 3, I think.

EK: Yes. It's kind of a quite silly game.

MW: Well, right, I mean, when 50 Cent is involved, and for some reason he has to go to the Middle East, then yeah ...

EK: Yes. Quite a ridiculous plot.

Anyway, there, I had a technical designer role, so there was a lot of working on game systems and getting deep into combat systems and like all the kind of tools that were used by the designers. So it was fairly technical. And I'd say it was less creative than the last job, which I wasn't too happy about. But it was just sort of how that team was structured, really. Also, we had quite a tight timeline. And there wasn't a lot of scope to do much creative, really.

But that was definitely an interesting project. 50 Cent threw quite a few spanners in the work [wrenches in the gears, for our US readers]. So yeah, basically he had some input into the game in the sense of … We sort of had this agent that we liaised with, and then this agent would kind of tell us different things that 50 Cent would randomly want. So the storyline to begin with was this, sort of like, it was basically like 50 Cent kind of in *Three Kings*, as it were, that movie back then.

MW: Yeah. So, to give you an anecdote that's similar regarding working with celebrities. When Volition was working on *Saints Row: The Third*, Burt Reynolds was in that, and for some insane reason, Burt Reynolds had very specific things that his character must not do. And I mean he was okay with everything. Like you could make it so that he was cursing or whatever, but he would not use a gun under any circumstances and he couldn't be lit on fire.

EK: Right. That must be quite tricky.

MW: Well, so, to this day, if you go back and play *Saints Row: The Third*, Burt Reynolds will beat enemies to death, but he will not equip a gun except for in some very particular circumstances. And even if you start a massive inferno, everyone else will burn to death, but he will not burn.

EK: That is hilarious.

MW: Yeah, just insane. Bizarre. Anyway …

EK: Yeah, this was similar, but it was more kind of throwing massive spanners into production.

So first of all, there was the whole thing of the story just being kind of insane, and politically questionable, but then …

MW: Sure. Yeah. [laughs]

EK: Later, we must've been at least two-thirds through the game, maybe even three-quarters, I don't remember exactly, but he suddenly … Like, the agent comes on saying—oh, 50 Cent was recently watching the movie *Blood Diamond* and really enjoyed the car chases in it, and we'd really like to get driving parts in the game.

We're kind of like, yeah, this is a third-person action adventure and there are currently no vehicles.

MW: [laughs]

EK: There is no way this will fit into the schedule. But unfortunately, we couldn't say no. There was no negotiation. But on top of that, he also wanted a helicopter in the game, like you the player flying the helicopter.

So this is, yeah, this was obviously like absolutely crazy because we had a deadline to hit and these were just massive asks.

MW: Right.

EK: So, we had to make a driving section of the game, which was, I think it was just one level in the end, which required, you know, like a lot of bespoke technology and art and everything. And we were using Unreal Engine at the time. So, you know, just a lot of stuff just wasn't … There was no way we could do a flying helicopter. Like, completely impossible to do that in time. So we had to do this kind of on rails shooting section with a helicopter that was literally the only thing that there was time to do.

I actually got the task of doing that level with the helicopter.

MW: Oh …

EK: Yeah. That was … I mean, it was fun to kind of work under mega-tight constraints with very limited support, and actually cobble something together. It's one of the most hacked-together things I've ever worked on. It was just absolutely bonkers.

Anyway, we somehow managed to ship that game. And, again, I think it's listed as a cult classic, because that's kind of … not the most highly rated game, but a lot of people sort of seem to talk fondly of it.

MW: That phrase. I've heard that phrase now from every single person I've interviewed which is, "and then somehow we managed to ship that game."

EK: Yes. That is definitely a common theme.

But anyway, I wasn't actually very happy living in Birmingham and I wanted to work on something more creative. I wanted to work on more interesting projects. I was just feeling a bit low. I think it was also because I'd really enjoyed the experience on *Call of Cthulhu* before.

But before the end of *50 Cent*, the end of development, there was actually an opportunity that popped up very randomly to help out on a project in Russia. It's a game called *TimeShift*, which was being developed by Saber Interactive. And they needed some help on trying to ship, because the game was going through a ginormous overhaul. Vivendi was the publisher. And they basically just sent a bunch of people from loads of different studios to go out to Russia to help bring up the quality of the game and then get it shipped.

And yeah, they just asked if anyone from Swordfish studio wanted to go. I'd never worked abroad and I just thought ...

Well, it sounds like an experience. I was keen on the idea of travel—a friend of mine had got back from working in California, in San Diego. And he was raving about it, saying, oh, amazing weather, and super good fun, and amazing experience. You've got to try something like that.

So that's what had got me excited about working abroad. But when they said it was Russia I thought—hmm ... Russia, that's probably going to be cold, and yeah, I might wake up one day in a bathtub of ice with my kidneys removed.

MW: [laughs]

EK: That was literally the reason someone gave as to why they didn't want to go. Like, there was another guy that was meant to go that pulled out the last minute because of just being scared about various dangerous things.

But anyway, I was umm-ing and ahh-ing about it, and I remember, the guy that ran the company, just came into the office one day, or came into my office and said—oh, Ed, so, you're all signed up for this Russia thing, that's brilliant to hear, yeah, so if you could bring your passport in tomorrow that would be ace, OK, thanks, bye.

And then all could say was—ah, OK, fine.—so I went to Russia. Let's just risk it.

So yeah, I ended up going to Russia for six months. It actually was an incredible experience.

Yeah, it was brilliant. The actual work was insane. I think we were working six days a week and often, you know, 10-, 11-, 12-hour days, like it was some crazy overtime. Because we were just desperately trying to get that game done. Yeah, just crazy, crazy kind of decisions in terms of chopping things and cutting things and changing things, just to get that thing done.

But it was a really fun experience. Russia was so different. And just a completely crazy place to be. I mean I could probably talk for hours about Russia itself. But yeah. It was pretty insane. I was staying in St. Petersburg. It was a very interesting experience. Definitely.

MW: That definitely sounds wild. I have never been to Russia. I've certainly seen a lot of the world. But that's not one that I've ever gotten a chance to touch.

EK: Well, um, it's probably quite different now as well. Apparently, when I went there, it changed a lot in the past five years. That's what everyone kept telling me. I think it's changed loads since as well. But yeah, great experience. And then I came back from that, and just really had this desire to travel, and to just go somewhere completely different, really.

And I had my eyes set on the US, on California. Just because, I looked through kind of all the different games companies I would really be into working for, and almost all of them were in California at the time. That's where AAA was really big. That was where the biggest companies were. I applied for a bunch of jobs in the US. Didn't get anywhere at all, even though I had some friends from the US that had worked with me in Russia and had given good recommendations, but it was always the same story about—oh, you don't have a visa or a green card, we're only employing people that are based here—and so on. Just no luck at all.

But eventually, I started to look elsewhere apart from the US, and a job popped up in Barcelona, in Spain, at a company called Grin, who had worked on *Bionic Commando.*

MW: OK. Oh, I love that, actually, that's like one of my favorite PlayStation 3 downloadable titles.

EK: Yeah. So that company was in Sweden, but they had a Spanish office, so I ended up getting a job there. That that was probably about a year that lasted for. Well, it might be less, it might have been about nine or ten months. We were working on a game called *Wanted,* so that was the game of the movie, basically. Sort of an action-adventure shooter kind of thing. This is kind of where you start to see a pattern … It's slightly self-imposed, and it's also based upon just—you get a bit of experience in a particular genre and then other companies will really want to hire you to work on a similar kind of game. Right?

MW: Yeah. I'm pretty much on … My personal brand that I've kind of been pigeonholed into is sort of open world chaos, crazy glib humor. So, *Saints Row,* that kind of thing. Absolutely. So everywhere I go in the games industry, there's like a specter of hookers and dildos and drug dealers and goofy, like, it's all just following me now. So this, I don't think it's even going to be possible for as long as I live now to work on something serious. Like, I don't think it'll ever happen.

EK: That's funny. No, that's just the way it goes. And it's good in some ways because it means if there is a job that meets your specialty, you can very easily get it, usually, but the amount of available jobs for that specialty obviously becomes smaller, right. Just by the nature of being a specialist I guess, or specializing.

MW: Sure.

EK: Anyway, so I went over to Barcelona, I absolutely loved living there. It was just the kind of change I needed. It was just a brilliant, amazing city.

But yeah, working at Grin was not so enjoyable. That was probably one of the worst experiences of my career. That was difficult for a bunch of reasons. It was a mega-tight deadline. So again, just loads and loads of crunch. And it's one of those things where I've accidentally established a pattern for a lot of my career, which is basically—start working on a game, finish it, company collapses, have to get out from under the job, go and work somewhere else, starting again partway through and rushing to ship it all over again.

And often a company is sort of like—oh, we need to get this done, oh, that's not quite right, oh, let's hire a designer, we'll get it all fixed up—so that's happened a lot. Then you sort of scramble onto a project, work a bunch of overtime, get the thing shipped. Try to correct the design as much as you can, but always wishing that you could have been there from the beginning. And then the game ships, the company runs out of money, and the cycle repeats.

MW: [laughs]

EK: That has happened to me a lot. Anyway, that's exactly what happened on *Wanted*.

I won't go into all the details of why that was so horrendous working there, but let's just say it wasn't an ideal situation.

MW: I understand.

EK: We had a very short time frame and not a lot of experience on the team. So that shipped, did OK, but pretty middling sort of average reviews, really.

And then I think the other game that they just released, which I believe is *Terminator Salvation*. And then I think actually, *Bionic Commando*, the 3D version, they all just didn't do as well as the company had hoped and that's why all these publishing deals that they had at the time just started to fall through.

That was it. After about nine or ten months suddenly—in Barcelona and really enjoying living there, but with suddenly no job. And unfortunately with very, very little in the way of game development at the time in Spain, let alone Barcelona itself, there weren't a lot of companies. So I was faced with that decision of, OK, what do I do? Do I go back to England? Do I try to stay here? Do I go somewhere else?—and I ended up actually getting a job at Epic Games Poland. So Epic bought People Can Fly, who had made *Painkiller*, and made this Epic Poland Studio. They were working on a game called *Bulletstorm*. I ended up going over there and that was just brilliant. Basically. Because I chose that project really carefully. So I saw the vertical slice in the interview, I was just like, this looks amazing. Also, just working with Epic as well just seemed to be ... It felt like it would be a great opportunity.

MW: Yeah. Certainly, Unreal Engine, *Gears of War* ... Yeah.

EK: It was exceptional.

So that was actually a lead designer role. So that was my first proper lead design position. It was brilliant. Really enjoyed working on the game. I think it was probably about two years or so. Just had a great time. And Poland was really good fun as well. Warsaw was great. I mean I'd already had a bit of a taste of sort of working abroad and also being in Russia. Some parallels there, although Poland is pretty different in a lot of ways.

But I really enjoyed it. And working there was great. We collaborated a lot with Epic and they were just super professional and really helped get the quality bar up really high. Gained tons of support. We had the regular calls with them to go through things and yeah, just learned a ton. And also from the guys at People Can Fly as well. Adrian, now, he has this indie studio called Astronauts, who worked on uh, *Ethan Carter*—was it?

MW: Yeah. *The Vanishing of Ethan Carter.*

EK: That was it. Yeah.

And now he's working on some "Witch" game, I think. But I learned a ton from him as well. And just really enjoyed it. That was a nice experience. Once we'd finished *Bulletstorm*—unfortunately, a sort of similar thing, game did not sell as well as they hoped. It was probably one of the best-reviewed games I have ever worked on, but it was at that point where AAA had started to become a bit messy, a bit dangerous.

Like, it was a point where you needed to be selling a lot of copies to be actually making a decent profit. Because it was like game development costs had gone up so high that you couldn't just sell a million copies and be like, yeah, cool, success—it was starting to really get a lot higher than that.

It was a real shame, to be honest. Because the game did turn out really well. That was one of the most creative games I have worked on. And just being a designer on it was just awesome. There were so many cool things in that game. So many cool mechanics. It was brilliant. But unfortunately, it just didn't have the success that they wanted it to, really, or they were hoping it would.

But that was fine because we had the support of Epic, and we then started working on *Gears of War: Judgment*. And, all was good; all was fine. I wasn't looking for anything new really at the time, but completely randomly, I got some email on LinkedIn from LucasArts Singapore, just saying they were looking for a designer at LucasArts Singapore … no, no, not really, thanks. But I've always kind of had an interest in working for LucasArts in San Francisco. I just kind of pretty much wrote that just randomly, almost half joking. But then the recruiter got back and said, oh, yes, we are actually looking for someone in San Francisco. Would you be interested?

I couldn't believe it. Like, yes, definitely. I think I even asked about the whole visa thing early on just to see, like, to make sure. And they were like, oh no, that's fine, we'd sort that all out. So one thing led to another, you know, had a bunch of interviews, went over there, was completely blown away. And as I was saying before, it was sort of my dream to work in California. But also complete dream to work on a *Star Wars* game at LucasArts. That was just too good to be true. I mean, I knew about the reputation of LucasArts from like the last—at the time, it was sort of the last few years before that, there was a lot of layoffs that happened several times—and the company definitely had gone through some troubles. But everyone was sort of reassuring me that that was in the past, and they had a really positive vision for the future. They'd had a lot of hires that really understood games and they were really doing some good stuff. And so I sort of took the leap of faith. And as I say, it was just too good to pass up. Just the opportunity to work in the US. And also for LucasArts.

So I said goodbye to Poland and went to San Francisco, basically.

MW: OK.

EK: That was an amazing experience as well. I was working on a prequel to *Battlefront* for about two years and we were really close to shipping. But then that whole Disney thing happened, basically. Like Disney took over LucasFilm and just decided they weren't interested in console games—development in house that is. They canned our project, and that was the end of that, unfortunately.

MW: Got it.

EK: Still, it was an amazing experience working there. There's so many perks. They would have these actors would come in and directors would come in and give talks. They had different classes for art or photography or filmmaking, story writing, all kinds of stuff. And then like, you know, phenomenal offices in the Presidio in this huge park in San Francisco. Everything was just insanely good.

But, unfortunately, that dream did not last. So that was a real shame. At that point, I didn't really want to leave San Francisco. I was sort of—what do I do next? Right.

That was probably the point where I started to really get a bit disillusioned in AAA, because it just happened so many times that the game I had worked on just hadn't done as well as I'd hoped for, and then that caused me to have to move jobs.

And also, we were so close. I couldn't believe it, that we have this game that we—we were playtesting it every day, because it was multiplayer mostly, and it was great. People really enjoying it. It was basically ready to ship and they just literally threw it in the trash, and you were just like, I can't believe this. That cost money to make and you're literally just throwing it away. It would cost very little to finish up. There's no way you wouldn't make your money back. And then some.

And just, lots of crazy decisions high up in that company as well, that kind of, I don't know, it all started to make me think like, do I really want to continue in AAA? The way it's headed, that companies just want these absolute mega, giant titles that have everything, you know, single player, multiplayer, co-op, open world, micro-transactions, whatever it is, just really stuffed full of features, in order to keep people playing for as long as possible. So they don't take the game and trade it in, or they don't sell the game secondhand or whatever.

MW: Right.

EK: So that was where AAA was going. And I just thought—do I really want to be there?

I did look at a lot of jobs in AAA, and I was interviewing at Arkane to work on *Dishonored 2*; I was interviewing at BioWare for *Mass Effect*; I was interviewing at Treyarch for *Call of Duty*. So I had a bunch of places that were good jobs, and good roles, in fairly interesting projects. I was pursuing those paths.

But then I basically just realized that I actually just want to try and go indie, and just try a different path.

MW: This is where you made the switch then? Right at this point?

EK: Well, not fully, though. Because I ended up working for a company called Dynamighty, which was just 10 people working on a game called *CounterSpy* in San Francisco. So that really was very random how that all came about. I just happened to see that company listed in a sort of recruitment fair thing that LucasArts had organized. I was very organized about just looking for different companies and seeing what was out there, really, and I just happened to spot them, and get in touch, and just kind of connected with the main guy, David Nottingham, and just, one thing led to another and eventually ended up getting a job there as a lead designer, because they were looking for someone to really, well basically, fix the design, and get the game done.

Again, so probably the exact same thing that I'd been doing for the past 10 years before. But it was a totally different shift, though, in terms of scale. From like a 60-, 70-, 80-person team to like basically 10 people.

MW: That's an interesting change from the previous roles, though, right? That had to be quite a significant shift.

EK: Absolutely. And that was sort of me deliberately trying to just kind of avoid this issue of … putting your future in the hands of big companies that were handling mega, mega big projects, that were becoming just so big and so volatile as well, in terms of just what we needed to succeed and so on.

I worked on *CounterSpy* for about a year. And really enjoyed being in a smaller team and I started to get into a little bit of programming. I was lead design of that, but everyone kind of looks in on everything in a small team.

MW: Yeah, indies kind of do a lot of everything, for sure.

EK: So I started to get into doing a bit of programming and really enjoyed it, because I hadn't really touched programming for years. So, unfortunately … This totally sounds like the repeating theme here, but *CounterSpy*, we shipped it, it came out, did not do as well as we'd hoped in terms of sales, and unfortunately the company didn't really have any runway to keep going because we'd put all our energy into that one game rather than securing the next deal because we were so sure we were going to work with Sony again, and they'd given us the indication. So that was the case. But they decided to downscale in terms of how many indie developers they were going to publish at that point. And unfortunately, we just ended up without a publisher, and not really enough money to keep going. So unfortunately, the same thing happened again, really. Just the company closed down.

So at that point, the guys at Dynamighty were kind enough to get me fixed up with some contract work at Gree, a mobile company, just to kind of see about figuring out what to do. And then I also worked at Zynga. Only for a short time. Just for about six months because basically I had an opportunity there that could have been quite interesting, because a friend of mine had started a—we were starting a team now, basically. And it looked like an opportunity to kind of actually work on something original from scratch. But unfortunately, it just didn't turn out like that. They company had already pivoted, by the time I got there, to what they were trying to achieve. And I just ended up working on about three projects that all got canceled in a row. So it was just—

MW: Oh, no.

EK: But it was enough time to kind of figure out what I really wanted to do.

I looked at a bunch of options for just all different—what were the options continuing in AAA and what did that look like? And in all honesty, I just could not find a project that I was super interested in and a role in that project that was what I wanted.

MW: Sure.

EK: There were certainly some interesting opportunities here and there. But again, just having to move from San Francisco, and I thought to myself, basically I'm in the city that apparently has the most video game companies in the world.

MW: Yeah.

EK: That's the statistics of San Francisco, right?

MW: Sure.

EK: And it looks like I might need to move. Like, the job that I want, to just continue, like, working as either a lead designer or design director or something like that, on a AAA project. And I thought—this is ridiculous; I can't be anywhere more safe than San Francisco [in terms of games]. So the fact that I might have to move to just get a job that I would want, it made me think that like, this is crazy. And even then all the jobs that I looked up were all like, sequels, prequels, franchise, continuations, just nothing that was like creatively inspiring. So that was one of the big things that made me—pushed me in the direction of trying to go indie by myself.

MW: OK.

EK: That, and a bunch of people ... At the time, I had various friends that were trying out the indie thing or at least friends of friends. A few people said to me—why don't you do it? You have design experience and you've now got programming experience, at least a little bit.

So in my free time I was with Zynga, I just worked on a little prototype of a kind of a driving game where you parked cars. It sounds kind of terrible and never made it into something. But it was a useful project to just kind of like a learn a little bit about like—would I have enough programming skills to make a game?

MW: There's quite a lot of people I've spoken to that have something like that. I mean, even I did the same deal, working at PlayStation, I made a little coffee shop simulator game, kind of a silly thing. And yeah, exactly the same kind of sort of red flag where it's like, oh, I'm even spending my free time working on something creative because I don't feel like I'm doing anything creative at work anymore.

EK: Totally. Totally. And also, I learned Blender, just spent a few months doing tutorials. Again, it was just exploratory—is this even vaguely feasible to do something, do a project by myself. And I really enjoyed doing those little experiments. There was a bunch of things that all kind of aligned together, which just pushed me off the edge, really. Then there was this article that I read that really stuck in my mind and made me think about it, which was basically saying, it was kind of saying that a lot of people that are very analytical or smart and think about things a lot, they'll often see all the reasons not to do something risky. So, for instance, all the reasons not to make your own game or start your own company or whatever.

MW: Sure.

EK: Like, someone very bright will sort of see like, oh, this could fail because of this reason, and this could not work because of that reason, and, yeah, shouldn't do that—whereas someone that is more kind of careless and hasn't really thought things through, and might just be kind of like—oh, I'll just try it, just give it a go, got this crazy idea, I'll just do it.

This article just kind of made me realize that tons of people do that, and they get success. And in the sense that something like that might fail, but then they'll try again and maybe another crazy idea or risk, risking it again. And then eventually they'll hit something big. Whereas the Mr. Cautious kind of supposedly smart person who is sort of analytical and careful and so on, just won't do anything, and will never have that chance at sort of doing something really interesting. And I was like, flip, this is just so true. Like, I've seen it so much with different people I've worked with and so on, and I just thought like, OK, I should try something.

MW: That's an interesting point.

I'm kind of jumping around on the script a little bit, but one of the last questions I typically ask folks is like, if you were speaking to yourself in the AAA role, sort of in the past, if you could kind of speak through time and say—hey, Ed, sitting at company X having a really bad time, thinking a little bit about maybe doing something independent—what would you tell yourself?

EK: Yeah. That's the thing. I've not had many jobs where I've not been happy. There's been a few roles where I wasn't happy for a bit, and then a drastic change happened. But I thought for many years here—now, maybe I should do my own thing—but I always thought like, oh, it's so hard to find the right people to work with. I remember thinking that a lot. And maybe the few years before I did go independent, just thinking like, oh, which programmer would I try and work with? Most programmers you talk to say, oh, I've got my own projects on my own engine, and they'd be on the side of—why I do I need a designer?

There was a bunch of stuff where I was always putting barriers up, let's say. I think I've done things in the right way because I do feel that having the design experience now is super useful. I don't think I was ready before, to be honest. Just having the time to get back into programming and scratch up on some articles, this all helped, really.

So I ended up doing that. I moved from the US. I moved back to Europe. But I decided to do that because it was just a lot cheaper than living in San Francisco. Also, the fact that I was only on the work visa; I didn't have a green card. And trying to do all that would have been a massive pain and very expensive, not to mention just cost of living being almost twice as much in San Francisco.

So I just thought, let's do it. Going to go back, be a bit nearer home, see my family more and just give it a go, basically. So that's what I've been doing for the past two years.

MW: Can you describe sort of what you're working on? Or the kinds of things do you do now?

EK: So I've been working for almost two years now, on a game called *Hang Line*. It's about swinging up mountains with a grappling hook, and getting kicked by angry goats. And this was me trying my best to kind of have a go at making a small simple mobile game. And just getting experience in the indie development process. And then completely failing at that in the sense of—I wanted to make a game in about three to six months. Spent two years on it. So that didn't go to plan.

But it was really starting to get very hard, because I've been working by myself on the game for nearly two years. It was getting pretty lonely and quite tough, and just total anxiety of not knowing where this was going, not knowing if the future was going to be working on games independently or me going back and getting a job. But just had no idea where things were headed.

But then, just recently in the past few months, basically I soft-launched the game in India to get some base data. It suddenly got picked up by pirates, got pirated all over, particularly in Russia and China—went insane in China; like about half a million pirated downloads. Then a company, a publisher, picks it up. Well, a bunch of publishers just had got in touch around this point. But it was actually one publisher in particular that I already knew about and had heard that they'd had good success and were really good for China. And China is a super-hard market.

MW: Yes.

EK: It is virtually impossible to penetrate China as an independent developer.

One thing led to another. They were just super interested in working with me and thought that this could be really huge. So now I've signed a deal with them, and we're now working on the game together.

MW: Great!

EK: So I've gone from complete unknown to just absolutely ... Now the comfort is that I'm going to be doing this for myself— and I've got the financial security now because I don't have to particularly worry that the game won't sell or anything. Because things happened to work out very favorably in that regard. And now the publisher, they've got a bunch of people working on it, too.

So my entire life has changed a lot in the past few months, basically. So that's been very positive.

MW: This is positive. I like to hear it, and I think you've kind of, just through the long narrative kind of hit most of my questions.

I guess I'll just leave you with—do you think it was a good decision overall? Would you do it again—moving away from AAA? And then anything else at all you'd like to add past that point?

EK: It's so hard to talk about in that way. Because honestly, if you spoke to me three months ago, we would be having a very different conversation. And I would be very, like, oh my goodness, what have I done? And so on.

Because you just have no clue with a game, whether it's going to be good or big or whatever. And like, you've got some ideas that some people enjoy it when they play it, but otherwise you're guessing.

MW: Right.

EK: But I've had friends that have lots of experience in games, have lots of friends of friends that I asked for advice and stuff. Lots of people telling me to just get it out; you've no idea if it will sell.

I obviously have been super lucky. And I think maybe part of that is just also being completely obsessed with quality and not being satisfied with just getting something out and it being a bit rough. That's sort of like almost a downside, I guess, because development ran much longer than I wanted, but it's become a plus side, because that's why this company got interested in it. That's why it's got potential.

So, would I do this again? Probably yes. Because I've had some success.

MW: Yeah.

EK: In terms of making games, I'm now committed to making games by myself and I should be able to do that. Unless something goes disastrously wrong over the next six months. But I'll be around as an independent developer for some time if this even goes vaguely well, basically.

I'm sorry, I've gone a little long here, I've really got to run.

MW: That's fine. What we love is a nice narrative of people's life changes. This is very much light reading. I'm not trying to push an agenda or advance a cause … I'd rather just provide something for people to read who are thinking of making a change themselves. So I think your narrative is quite helpful.

EK: OK, great.

MW: Perfect. All right, well I'll talk to you soon. Thanks so much for your time. I really appreciate it.

EK: No problem at all.

While not nearly as catastrophic as Ben's story, clearly Ed was growing frustrated with the work he was doing. Between licensed titles, celebrity cameos, and more, something just didn't feel right. I felt a kind of camaraderie with Ed during the interview—my workplace certainly didn't abuse me, and I didn't feel slighted, but fundamentally, something was just missing.

In the industry, unfortunately, continued employment often requires the game to gross a significant profit, and working in a speculative industry, employers can't often guarantee that kind of success. In Ed's case, game after game did poorly, or at least, was less successful than the publishers and developers intended. As a result, Ed had to hop from job to job, continent to continent. Recurrent themes in the interviews discuss stability, not having to move, and the desire to get back to doing something more creative.

When working in a creative medium that becomes less creative, making a change seems the next obvious choice. For both Ed and our next interviewee, Nigel, that meant going indie. For me, too.

Nigel Kershaw, previously Sony, Deep Silver, Ocean

I met Nigel when working for Deep Silver during a trip to England. I was headed over for a user research conference, and Deep Silver decided this would be a good time for us to get an analytics system in place for *Homefront: The Revolution*. Sadly, neither analytics nor my trip were enough to save that game. Nigel was working with

Dambuster as a contract employee at the time, part of his transition out of a traditional games role. Eventually, he'd make a foray into VR, and finally to full-time independent work.

MW: OK. Thanks for taking the interview—first question, can you introduce yourself how you'd like to be introduced?

NK: My name's Nigel Kershaw. I am a game designer by trade. I have been a game designer since 1989. So I've been a game designer for a very, very long time. I've always been a game designer. I didn't get into the industry by not being a game designer. I accidentally fell into the games industry by being a dungeon master in sort of role-playing games. And guys that I used to role-play with worked at a video game company making Spectrum games, Nintendo games, all that. NES stuff that actually that started on a Spectrum, and the boss there was fascinated by computer RPGs. So they said oh, we know someone can do that. And they hired me, and I've been a game designer ever since. So anyway, it's kind of a nontraditional access into the games industry. I've been doing it ever since. Actually, I've never not been a game designer.

MW: OK, cool. I'm going to ask you a couple of questions about your life in games. If you have to anonymize or omit anything that you can't share or are uncomfortable sharing, that's totally fine. NDA, stuff like that. You can also feel free to plug at length any game or project you're working on right now because as the book comes out, I will happily put it in there. All right, so question one, you've already kind of answered a little bit about this. How long have you been working in games ... if you could, uh, give me a little, brief kind of career rundown. Sort of how you got here.

NK: So you ready for this?

MW: Yeah, go nuts.

NK: I started working in video games in 1989 at a small local company called MagiTech based in a tiny little town in the UK, in Dewsbury, which is in darkest Yorkshire. It was a real small-town outfit, but it was a time when there were a lot of really talented coders coming up through the ranks of home computers, basically. So they were getting together and there was a lot of money to be made out of making these video games. It was sprites, it was really, really simple stuff. So this company kind of grew over time. It worked out for a few years. I made a couple of, not brilliant but all right games, one called *Daemonsgate*, which is a sort of role-playing game, a not great, nice little sort of eight-bit RPG. And then I got a job at Ocean Software, the famous, if you're English, the famous sort of British-famous Ocean Software, which is, well, was a big publisher through the eighties in the UK.

MW: Okay.

NK: Right, 90s when they were looking to expand, games were getting more expensive to be made and they were looking to solve … you know, effectively, I think directors wanted to get out of Ocean, and they wanted to sell out because it was getting expensive and very, very corporate. The easy days of making money in games was over. So they wanted to ramp up Ocean, make some big gains, but also, at the same time, this made the company look attractive to a buyer, basically. So I was kinda hired on to … the brief was basically make an epic game, go away and make us an epic game, do whatever you want. And I was in my early 20s at the time. I knew nothing about how to make games and I was like a dog with two dicks, you know. I mean, it was brilliant.

I ended up making a game called *HMS Carnage*. Right. *HMS Carnage* was a sort of 3D action game. Kind of like 3D action, flying, driving … you have tanks, you have planes, it was set on Mars in a steampunk, Victoriana-type universe. And we decided that we were gonna do loads of FMV. FMV was a big thing at the time, so we thought, all right, let's do FMV in there—

MW: Oh, like *Wing Commander.*

NK: Yeah, that kind of thing. So we basically, to cut a long story short, we hired a film production company. We got loads of actors in. We did like 12 hours of blue-screen filming. I think it was the most expensive film shoot in Manchester at that point and the company bought an Onyx Silicon Graphics machine. Big expensive hardware. Basically, we thought we were on the money to just make this awesome game, but it was completely overambitious, completely over the top, not a bankable IP. It was basically very British, there were a lot of cricket references in there. It's all sort of very Britannia, pip, pip, tally ho, and stuff like that about it all, it was brilliant, we loved it, and then basically Ocean got bought by Infogrames.

Infogrames, being French, just didn't get it. Well they did get it, they did get the fact that it was completely overambitious. They also didn't get the very Englishness of it. They're like, well how do we sell this, you know, I mean it was very, very British. So they closed it down and they closed down *HMS Carnage* very, very rapidly after we got bought out. But ultimately, it did what the directors of Ocean wanted it to do. It made Ocean look like we were all in the big time.

MW: Got it. Okay. Fake it until you make it sort of thing.

NK: But obviously, I was responsible for this whole debacle, so I didn't see any of the money out of it. I just made it to do it.

So anyway, that was a good learning experience. It really taught me a lot about how just not to make games in a way … you know, just never underestimate the logistics of this shit because it's just, it's insane, you know what I mean? Ever since, it's always been a part of the games process for me is all about constraints. So about setting constraints on what you're going to do before you start so you don't go batshit insane and spend loads of money and then end up with 12 hours of blue-screen FMV footage that I still have on a VHS upstairs. I just couldn't resist anyway, but I still wanted to be a game designer. From there, I bummed around for a little while, I went to work at Psygnosis as a game designer. I think this is when game design was starting to be a thing.

It wasn't just the one guy putting together endless documents that nobody reads. This was more rigging levels, scripting levels, putting gameplay together, you know what I mean? As sort of a member of the team, instead of the man in the high castle. I learned my trade as a game designer doing those sort of things. So I was at Psygnosis, after Psygnosis I went to Particle Systems, did a lot of space games, really enjoyed that 'cause there was a lot of scripting involved in that. A lot of actually constructing gameplay, and then building it up over time, and then, I ended up at a startup called Brain in a Jar where we basically wanted to do racing games.

I don't find racing games fun. I despise racing games. But, I ended up working on racing games. I did eight in a row, I did eight racing games in a row. So the first one, was ... Brain in a Jar, we did Indy cars, we did the *Indy 500*, basically, and it was all right, but there's only so much you can make interesting about a game where you just turn left.

MW: I mean, if you're going fast enough, you don't really even turn left. You just kind of drive straight, not to belabor the point.

NK: I kind of got into it, but I hate racing, I hate motor racing. Right. And I don't like racing games, but over time I did eight in a row. I've learned to like making them, if that makes sense.

MW: This sounds a bit like being a sushi chef with a shellfish allergy.

NK: Yeah, yeah, yeah. By the time I got to Evolution and Sony times, I'd be working on *MotorStorm*. But that was after doing rally games and stuff like that. I got into the "gamey"-ness of these things and I think *MotorStorm* was kind of part of bringing that "gamey"-ness in there, bring a bit of OK, you know, you're all in different vehicles, you've got different routes, pick your route sort of thing and turn it into almost like a puzzle game.

... It didn't quite work, but the experience was really good and it taught me a lot about smoke and mirrors in games, and how people read a lot more into it than what's actually there, you know? And *MotorStorm* was really successful, a PlayStation launch title. Sony bought Evolution Studios, we made *Pacific Rift*. And then I was part of the Sony system. So I ended up as game director on most of *Pacific Rift*, which was really good. And then I kind of became ... I kind of ended up in that corporate middle ground, you know where you're promoted to your level of incompetence.

MW: Yes, yeah, very familiar with that.

NK: Yeah, yeah, yeah. So I ended up in a position where I was like … I wasn't making games anymore. I was … I was too far removed. I was many, many steps removed from the floor and was effectively powerless to influence anything. You know what I mean? You're in an advisory role in this kind of wasteland of corporate executives where nobody wants to make a decision.

MW: I will say that this is not the first time, in the process of writing this book or otherwise, that I have heard almost that exact sentence.

NK: Right, yeah. 'Cause to me, like making a game, the stuff I enjoyed about making the game, was being on the coal face. Was making those decisions … playing it, holding the game, and making those decisions and getting things done and making things happen. Because gameplay is all about iteration, I mean fast iteration, you never get it right the first time around.

You've gotta play with it, you've gotta feel it, you've got to touch it, you got to experience it and then you've gotta change it to make it better. But when you're in this executive soup, you can't effect any real decisions, you can't do anything at all … and everybody ends up being so … "how high up the food chain can I get?" It all becomes about being an executive rather than making games. You know what I mean? Then there's politics and everyone's out to please everybody else, nobody wants to make a decision because if you make a decision and it's a bad idea, then that reflects badly upon you because you were the one who had the idea, and … you know …

… I hated it. I hated every moment of it.

So, basically, I left Sony about 2011. I was made redundant, because I was just one of the big mouths who weren't that useful, but I'd also been there quite a while. So I walked away with a nice slab of cash in my pocket, the severance pay in the UK, it was quite good. Back at the time, the severance package was quite good, you know what I mean? So then I thought … well what the hell do I do now? I knew I was miserable doing what I was doing, but that's all I'd done for quite a few years. So I thought, OK, what's the industry doing now? Because when you're in that AAA thing, you can get isolated from the world about you, you know what I mean?

You're in a sort of corporate machine, inside of a corporate comfort blanket, that sort of cocoon. And then soon you're out in the wilds, and I never really did much sort of outreach-y stuff, I didn't do much lecturing, and stuff like that while I was there, you know what man, I kept my interest constant, and as I searched, it looked like a very empty space.

And I thought, what the hell? I'm not going to jump into another job doing what I was miserable at. I was gonna make things again. So I'm going to do what I did when *HMS Carnage* failed. I basically just got a job being a game designer for hire. I can make games. I can put those bits of gameplay together for you. And I did.

I can sit there, I can work from a list, I can write lists, I can do all that sort of stuff. And I did all right at that. I got back in a few gigs, doing point-and-click adventure games. Again, it's very scripted, so it's pretty much the design and writing, you sit there and you write the game. I got to know Charles Cecil at Broken Sword, director of Revolution. And so I ended up working on *Broken Sword 5*, a big point-and-click game, the Kickstarter one. Small team, a lot of work and, and so on and so on and so on ... I got by. And then a couple years ago, I worked with some friends at Sony to do a startup where they wanted to do a VR game. So I went from point and clickers into sort of VR strategy games.

MW: I played that VR game, that was *Tethered*, right? When I was at Sony, I was working with the PSVR headset, so I plugged your game to everyone in the office.

NK: Oh, and the numbers stuff, the data stuff when we met—that was just another one of these gigs where I was hired on for a big AAA game, I did my job, and then I went away sort of gigs, you know what I mean? The problem with all those sort of gigs, they're really good, but basically you're away from home quite a lot. Because they're the big studios they're kind of remote around the UK. It was pretty much OK, I'm going down to this drafty little bed that I rent during the week, and then I'm home on the weekend.

MW: I think you told me about this when we were in Nottingham, that you had some rather grand commute to get back to where you were.

NK: Yeah, I have a little cottage in the countryside. I bought my house. It's actually quite close to where Sony used to be, but I like my house. I've got a bit of land, a tiny little cottage, all placed in the countryside. I love it, and so, I don't want to move. I don't want to because I could've taken another big corporate job and pulled up sticks and emigrated to Canada, or Sweden, or anywhere like that. But I'm very much happy now and quite settled here.

MW: Yeah, exactly. I mean, where you see me right now is the basement of my house in Pennsylvania. I mean this is where my wife's from. This is home for me. I get it.

NK: Yeah. You lay down your roots. I'm comfortable with that, but it just means you've got to take work wherever it comes. You know what I mean? With the freelance stuff I've done all right. I got five … No, I got more than five, I got like six or seven good years out of it, basically doing loads of different interesting projects sometimes for a couple of days, sometimes for a couple of years. Which brings me around to now.

So now another old colleague of mine, a few old colleagues, actually, from the *MotorStorm* days at Sony. We got together after *Tethered* failed. So the VR stuff, it just didn't sell. I mean, *Tethered* was a great little game, I thought, it was interesting and I thought VR was fascinating, but I also struggled quite a lot with it. Because basically, a lot of my game design paradigms that I used for years just didn't really work in VR.

MW: I'm having a lot of trouble with the concept of game design for VR generally. It makes for some very unique, interesting challenges to not make a game that's essentially a gimmick of the technology, right?

NK: Yeah. Exactly, I think we were in a position where as a designer, I'd love to learn more about this, but in a commercial environment, they're small AA indie games, you know what I mean? And I think VR for me now is working on these kind of smaller games with a reasonable budget with high production values or stuff like that. I want someone else to spend the shitload of money in failures and research to truly understand what good game play is like in VR. I don't have the time nor the money to actually figure that sort of shit out. It's interesting. Fascinating. I would enjoy going back into it again if someone said, right, go away and do something in VR here with a big sack of cash. You know what I mean?

MW: Absolutely. OK, cool. So I was going to go on and ask you how you got your start in the games industry, but you sort of already answered that one. So, the next two questions, I mean, you kind of touched on these as well. I would typically ask you what made you want to make the jump from traditional AAA, and I think you've kind of touched on that a little bit with the ... sort of the corporate dissatisfaction? I mean that's ...

NK: There was that ... it was really realizing that when I came out of Sony I'd been miserable in the corporate thing, and that I'd lost touch with the hands-on, actual tangible making of games. But by going back and actually just freelancing as a designer, I'd come in, do your stuff, make gameplay for you. It reaffirmed the joy that I get from that, I remembered that I enjoy doing it. I realized that actually, the farther I am away from the actual game, the less interested in it I am.

But also from when I was game directing, I enjoyed having that perspective of shaping the overarching thing that we were making as well, but still that means a small team ... that means a small, tight team of good people where everybody knows what they're doing. That, to me, that's the sweet spot. That's the absolute sweet spot of making games.

So, don't get me wrong, I might go back to do AAA stuff like that, but probably not. I turned down a few gigs over the past few years while I was freelancing, twice, like something that would basically double my salary to go do a big corporate gig somewhere else in the country. So I'd have to move, but again, I can't be bothered. I know I'd be miserable.

MW: About a week after I got back from California, back to Pennsylvania, someone tried to hire me at a very large mobile game company in San Francisco. Data science stuff is really big right now for reasons neither I, nor I think anyone else, really understands. And so it's very frequent that I get, like, LinkedIn recruiter calls and things like that. It was really interesting because that same thing, you know, someone had offered this bucket of money and I had to politely tell this recruiter, I just drove 6000 miles to get out of California. Man, I don't see me packing up and coming back anytime soon.

NK: Absolutely. I don't want to say it's because I can't be assed. It's not like I'm lazy about it. It's just I know that yes, there will be financial reward for it, but I can forego that financial reward for actually enjoying what I'm doing. So I would just spend my existence doing performance reviews or whatever else. You know what I mean, it's like, wow, great.

MW: This next question here, a lot of people have really interesting stories here and you can feel free to share something if you want to, and you can not if you don't. I open this book talking about me getting a haircut. And there's a reason for this. At PlayStation in San Diego, they would pull a barber in a trailer onto the campus to the studio because you didn't have time really to go do things like that. Like you didn't have time to get downtown.

I'm not sure if PlayStation actually hired the barber or not, or if it was just the corporate park that PlayStation was located in, but regardless … The traffic was atrocious. You were there your eight to eleven hours a day, there is no reality where you are going to get your haircut. Seems a little inane, but this struck me kind of suddenly.

So it was get your haircut in the parking lot in the back of a fifth wheel, or look like a caveman. And so I just had this sort of moment of absurdity where I thought, I am literally having a company-sponsored haircut because I don't have time to do even this most basic human thing in my life anymore. Between the city and the job, those things are just gone.

That was a bit of a tipping point for me to be like, OK, you know what? This isn't what I wanted out of games. This isn't a good way to live life. So the question is if you had or remembered any kind of absurd moment, or breaking point, or sort of red flag moment where you thought, OK, you know what, this isn't just me malingering. This is not a thing I can do anymore. It doesn't have to be any one thing, but this has come up with some interesting anecdotes from other folks.

NK: Trying to think now because it wasn't the crunch bit.

MW: Yeah. I actually don't mind some crunch as long as I'm working on something I care about, like if I have a project that I really care about, like when we were working on *Agents of Mayhem*, which unfortunately didn't do super well, but like, when you're working on it and you like it, it doesn't feel so bad to be asked to work a little longer; that doesn't bother me so much.

    On the other hand, as a data guy, I'm a bit spoiled with regard to crunch. I generally don't get the brunt of it like a content creator would. More than that, it's just kind of the general lifestyle, I think that this had more to do with California and being in AAA generally than it did about Sony particularly. PlayStation was, all things considered, a great place to work. You know, I could've had that same experience at 3000 other companies in that area.

NK: Yeah. I mean, our crunches, we had it hard. And you probably shouldn't write this down …

MW: It's all right; again, you're getting first pass at this.

NK: Well, basically our decree, we had a hard core—on the *MotorStorm* games—we had a hard core of basically working-class British lads who were very talented in what they did, and had a very strong work ethic about them. But we were also "high" people. So there were a lot of drugs, a lot of boozing, a lot of rock and roll. It was almost like a rock-and-roll thing. At the time, it kind of felt a bit like a seventies British rock band type thing. You know what I mean? It was quite …

MW: This is kind of interesting, though—and again, I'm gonna transcribe this so you can do with it as you like before I publish it. This is kind of interesting, though, because you know it was at least a little bit that when I was at Volition, right? We had a giant six-foot penis on the wall, there's a margarita machine that wheels around to desks, more than a few of us had alcohol problems. I mean we were the company that shot strippers out of a cannon (in our games, to be clear). Things like this in games … I guess it just doesn't surprise me that much.

    Also, you know, in the wake of this whole Nolan Bushnell controversy at GDC, you know, the stories that are coming out about Atari now … what I'm saying, I guess, is that the stories you're talking about, where is this very much like a booze, drugs, and rock-and-roll thing, are not uncommon in our industry, unfortunately.

NK: It's that rock-and-roll vibe … in our own way, I can see why Led Zeppelin did what they did. Or maybe there's something about the British psyche that basically turns it massive. We work really hard. But it turns into massive hedonists. It kind of worked, though. It worked for those games. But it was, well, it certainly wasn't that healthy, and to be honest, I'm glad in a way that I'm not doing that anymore because I would've burnt out after awhile. You know, I think a lot of people burn out, a lot of people.

It's a tricky one for me to come up with a specific anecdote, it was more just a general malaise, and it was almost like a hangover from this hedonistic rock and roll, we're making something awesome, railroad towards death or glory sort of thing … and then actually rising above that and not being allowed to do that again because they didn't do games like that anymore, if that makes sense. And then ending up in this kind of corporate soup of like … I just didn't enjoy it anymore.

MW: That's totally fine. Occasionally when I ask this question, people have a very specific moment where they're like, "I was on super crunch and I fell asleep in my car in the parking lot." Or they have these moments where they're very clearly like, OK, white flag, I'm done. I have to stop this.

NK: That's the thing, and it's the British attitude thing, 'cause I had all those moments. I slept in my car, I slept under my desk. I've been in the office for, like, days on end. You know, I've not had a day off for like six months sort of thing, but it was a buzz. I loved it. It was really a good time for me.

I guess it was once it became all about the money, I guess once it became about trying to turn our company into a hits factory, when it became about structures and hierarchies and what job title everybody had. Everybody became obsessed about what their job title was. Fuck that shit. You know, this is me and the corporate world, we just don't get on. I don't know what it is. I mean, I'm from a working-class socialist background, I have just a real problem with authority.

MW: I certainly can relate to that. You know, one of the lines in the book details that at some point I realized I was actively involved in making money more than I was in making games. And yeah, I think that that resonates with me quite a bit.

NK: Not only that, it was actually making some other fucker money.

MW: Yeah, that's fair. Boss gets a dollar. I get a dime. This is a pretty regular conversation across industries. Yeah. I was going to ask next, at the core of it, what did you find missing? But I think you kinda hit that, right? I'm not making games and that's not how I want my life to be, that's really the punchline. So if you want to refill your gin, this is probably a decent time.

NK: Helen, two seconds. Helen … could I have another gin please? Or a Scotch, maybe it's Scotch time …

MW: Or maybe both! Just mix it around in a giant bucket! All right. So logistics. Yeah. So the big question that everyone's going to have reading a book like this is: How did you do it? How does somebody who is right now, it doesn't have to be directions for someone else—

NK: Excuse me, two seconds, gin's arriving!

Helen: You stop swearing. He's Canadian and very polite.

MW: Hello! Charmed.

So. All right. So the next question is, then, how do you do it? You don't have to answer this question for everybody and, in fact, I'm sure you can't and that's fine. But basically, one of the things that everybody reading a book like this is going to think is, "maybe I'm not super happy," you know, maybe you have a super-talented animator or super-talented designer and they're sitting in Company X and they don't feel like they have enough impact and they want to do it for themselves.

Obviously, you can't answer the question for everyone, but people are curious as to how you actually walk out the door. Because, I mean, obviously you end up with financial problems. If you're in the United States, you end up with healthcare problems. There's a whole myriad of things that kind of go by the side of the road when you choose to walk out the double doors and turn in your badge. So how did you do it? How did it work for you to move to a little indie project from these sort of more reliable AAA income sources?

NK: Contacts. So, basically the first thing to do is sort of figure out what you're good at. Yeah. What can you do that is a bankable skill? What can you do that someone is willing to pay money for, and genuinely people are willing to pay money for an executive head of design resources or fucking whatever tangible physical, bankable skill you have. And mine was … well. Game design is such a nebulous fucking concept. Every fucker thinks they're a game designer, basically, and then they probably are.

But the secret of game design is that it's not about ideas. It's about presenting ideas, abstracting ideas, writing a big list that describes what an idea is, you know what I mean? But basically just get those talents out there. Don't try and look for the same job title that you have now. Don't try and look for the same money that you have now. It's amazing what you can do when you're saying, "Shit, right? OK. That subscription could go and that subscription could go" and just kind of keep what money you get from coming out of somewhere and just have three months' salary in the bank and that was it.

Once I'd gotten three months' salary in the bank, I was all right. And then you basically go and you find a job. The first job is really hard and might be a bit shit, but you just keep your head down, just keep doing it, keep doing it, then do another job, then do another job. But as you're doing these jobs, you get to know the companies who use freelancers. I needed to earn a living being a game designer, in this industry, and there's a lot of people who, basically, when they've got a crunch on, when they're closed in, they just need people who can make content. I can make content.

I did three months deleting trees, basically, for a very popular brand of racing game, and I knew a studio who was doing a conversion of that to the XBOX 360. The original was done on the XBOX One, they were doing the XBOX 360 version. The problem with the XBOX One is it's a much bigger system, so they have a lot of landscape trees in it. To make it work on XBOX 360, they had to get rid of a lot of those trees.

You couldn't algorithmically get rid of those trees because it looks shit. So you had to basically artistically—

MW: You spent three months cutting trees out of a game.

NK: It was brilliant because they need bums on seats just to do the mechanical shit, and when you're doing that mechanical stuff ... I found audio books. Literally put an audiobook on, and make trees look pretty. It's not exciting, but it paid the rent and then it got me to know people who, when you do a good job they ring you up and basically you end up getting to get into a core group of people who you see quite often, you work together and then kind of somebody else, he's got an in and you work with more people.

It's even just ... It's not necessarily the influencers that you wanna contact, it's the colleagues that you work with, people you were next to, they go onto another job and they say, oh, we need a game designer, I know someone who is really good. As long as you're good at doing that job, you will get a name out for yourself.

MW: The way you're saying contacts here is different than most books and topics in the games industry talk about contacts because, of course, most of our "breaking into the games industry" books say things like, "meet the recruiter at this place," "meet the CEO at this place," "meet the CFO at this place." But what you're talking about is like looking for other sort of "chums" who were in the same throes you are, the other folks that are deleting trees.

NK: Yeah, exactly. In some ways, it was a low point in my career and in other ways, it came on at perfectly the right time, maybe it was interesting stuff before and then interesting stuff after. But these jobs ... I found them by not being picky. It's just being in the system and earning money; it's fine. You know, the next thing will come along, and eventually I'd work myself into a position where it's like, all right, let's make a game, what game are we going to make, and we eventually got in a position where we could do that, but up until then, I just kind of had to earn my keep in game design and enjoy it, enjoy the simple things. You know, I mean there's a certain aesthetic beauty in placing trees on a hillside.

Even if you're doing the most mundane thing, even if you're writing lists or whatever, you're making some things, a craft. And at the end of the day, the sum is greater than the parts with a video game and even if you contribute to that in a small way, you can take a certain amount of pride in that.

MW: I will say that you've got a remarkably chipper outlook.

NK: Yeah. You've got to have that ... the game industry breaks a lot of people. I kind of just let it wash over me. You do have to be like "whatever, it's the fucking games industry." I've been here 28 years, man. It is a long time doing this shit it's well ... "hell of a new boss, same as the old boss," you know what I mean? Exactly the same problems come up. Exactly the same disasters every time.

MW: So how did it feel? Can you give me a little bit of a one, two punch on getting to the point where you can actually work on your own stuff, like a hundred percent, not deleting trees per se, but when you're actually like, OK, I want to make a game here. When was that moment? When did that come and what was sort of a payoff there? Did you think that you had made the right decision at that point?

NK: Yeah. So I had a couple of false starts in my career ... let's do a startup, let's make a game, and then it didn't happen. There are reasons, but logistically ... you need an office, you need space, you need to get together. You know, you need to pay people, you need to fucking pay people. Doing it for free, people get bored. And as soon as something that pays comes along, away they go. You have to pay people.

So back last year, Secret Sorcery and *Tethered* didn't bring in that much money. I did bits and pieces of freelancing for various people, consulting and stuff like that. And then I took a sabbatical. I took three or four months off, basically to spend some time just doing my own shit; my sister flew over from Australia, and stuff like that. And then I had money in the bank and I was like, all right, time to do just little things, and not worry about them. I got to that point when I thought, I don't have to keep three months salary in the bank because I know there's work out there if I go hunting for it. And it just so happened a good friend of mine, Alan, was like "All right, I have some funding, we want to start up a studio, we want to make a game, do you want to make a game, what game do you want to make?" Shit. So now we've got money and so we thought, right, OK, we can make a small game in a year or so, throw it out on the market and then see what happens. The thing with that sort of stuff is that the indie market is very crowded at the moment, there's so much shit out there. And the thing with games is you may have the best game in the world, but if people don't buy it, you're fucked.

MW: You can't find it sometimes, let alone buy it … there very well could be, you know, I would, I would stake my life on the fact that there are probably 100 just absolutely game-of-the-year of spectacular indie games buried somewhere deep in the Steam catalog. That are just hidden in the cloak of invisibility.

NK: So we decided. You come up with a concept, we make a prototype. We do all the due diligence, we make a sales pitch, we write up game design documents, we'd get it all nice and tidy, and then we go whore ourselves to publishers. And normally we'd go get published and we go, right? It's kind of like an AA game. So basically, what we're looking for is that sort of middle ground, and I think the middle ground will be good because we're good at that. We've all made big games. And that's the takeaway from making big games is knowing how to put all the different pieces of this monstrosity together in time, and just as importantly how to cost all this shit out, right?

How much it's gonna cost, what jobs need doing, what people do we need to do these jobs, how much you're going to pay those people that do those jobs, what else needs doing and just coordinate and actually come up with a plan of how to put this thing together. It's not straightforward, but you know, you've done it for so long. I just know how these things fit together and can come up with a good pitch, a good demo, and then go to the publishers.

I never really did the whole "Oh I'm just going to make my game" thing, To me, the joy of making games is the joy of collaboration. I'm not a multitalented guy, I can't draw for shit. I'm not a brilliant coder, I can write all right scripts. I like to surround myself with good artists and good coders. To do that, you need to pay them because once you're paying them, everybody's got a vested interest in making it good, you know?

MW: Yeah. A lot of folks I've talked to about do a combination of pay and some small equity piece, so they'll be like, OK, you know what? We're paying you below the market average, but you're being paid enough to live, you're working on a thing that you like, and you have 10% of the company or whatever.

NK: This is precisely the sort of thing that I'm doing, and that's good in a way because it does turn you into enough of a businessman to get involved, you know what we're doing, it's not just a creative endeavor, it's got senses of a creative endeavor and a commercial enterprise, so it's not art, it's craft to a certain degree. It's like having a woodworking shop. Okay, I can make a chair now. You're going to make more money by doing 15 nice chairs a year than you are by just making your dream chair. The chair that you can spend 20 years making. It's a craft and it's sort of that having that realization that I have a stake in this company. If it is successful, I will be successful. How do you make games successful? It's very hard, but you have try and it's a dice roll, but you've just got to stack the dice in your favor as much as you can from experience.

MW: Would you describe your new venture? Like what the company is doing? You can plug away if you want to. Tell me about it. Tell me what you did, what you can. You don't have to give away the keys to the kingdom.

NK: So, three of us, myself of course, and Alan McDermott to do the business side of stuff and the game director stuff. He was the audio director on *MotorStorm*, and then this guy called triff, with a small case t, just triff. He's a good guy. He's a great artist, good mind on him, and a great 3D artist.

So we kind of thought, all right, let's do some things. So we formed the company, we thought, right, let's get some staff. We got a young coder that we know who's really, really talented, right. We need some bums on seats, so we thought, let's get some graduates. So we tout ourselves around the master's courses, all sorts of good universities around the country. And basically because during my freelance stuff, I'd done a lot of lecturing at university, so you get contacts and so you ring up your contact one day and say "Who's your best game design master's graduate, what's his name, what's his email address?"

We've got three amazing people that way—artist, designer, and coder, and they're all really good, and they bolster out the team … and it's good, it's giving people a leg up in industry, but it's teaching how you make games properly so they're getting something out of it, but at the same time you're getting talented staff at reasonable prices … and then you just go for it, so there's nine of us now and we've used a lot of freelancers that we know, like Alex Figini had been over at BioWare; he's now freelance, he's like a really good concept artist. We know a lot of people who are good animators, a lot of people we worked with on *MotorStorm*; the animator was doing some animation on *Thor*, and he's freelance.

While we've got a core team of nine people in the office, we've got this network of people who are good at doing what they do. We know they're good at what they're doing because we worked with them before and we're sorta putting all these bits together to basically make a demo for a new game I'm not gonna say anything about, because we've not announced it yet, but it's not a racing game.

MW: Ah, wonderful. There is the opportunity, if there comes a time where you do have an announcement, I can put a little edit in here and say, anyone reading should totally check out X, Y, Z.

NK: And that's the other side, it sounds arsey not to talk about it. We're trying to play the whole social side of stuff, the other side to making a game is basically getting that recognition. It's getting people to know who you are and what your game is, and what we're doing right now is letting the publishers and financiers know who we are and eventually we'll carry that through into trying to let the public know as well … because one thing that we failed to do effectively on *Tethered* was marketing, and it's really hard getting people to recognize you, to know what your game is and then go out and buy it. So you're kind of your own marketer as well, both in terms of marketing your company and marketing your product, and the earlier you start, the better.

MW: No, it's totally fine. You're not the first person who has said, "I'm working on a thing. I will tell you about it later." That's totally fine. I can put a little—

NK: As game developers we are super precious. It's quite funny where everybody always is really sort of precious about what they're doing. Nobody likes to be the first one just to sort of chat about, oh yeah, I'm doing this.

MW: No, I completely agree. I've worked contracting for some like, military subcontractors that are less secretive than game developers, which is sort of bizarre in its own way. But yeah, no, it's totally fine. Another question, and you can feel free to answer or not. How did the jump affect your financial situation? Has this been like a hard thing, or … You know, but basically just give me a little bit of insight on that. As much as you feel comfortable with, of course.

NK: It's less predictable. I'm in the fortunate and enviable position of, well I don't have kids. Me and my partner, we don't really. I don't really do kids. I like kids to borrow for a while. But that's it. So I don't have those family commitments. I have a partner who earns good steady money in a good steady job and I can earn big loads of money or I can earn shit all for three months, and as long as they're willing to sort of ride those peaks and troughs, it's fine, you know. We'll go on holiday in the tent in the wilderness this year rather than go to Spain. So no big deal.

So I certainly haven't hit the pinnacle of what I was earning at Sony, and never have done, but then, the time you spend in that sort of environment, you spend money to make yourself happy. And you get into a habit of just sort of having that life that, that sort of middle-class lifestyle of just a state of low grade excess, and I don't miss that. If I want something, I can get it. But I just like, oh, just save for that, wait a few months, and we'll get it. So you've just got to be a bit more old age pensioner, a bit more baby boomer about your finances I think. I guess I'm "Gen X" because I'm terrible with money.

MW: OK. But that's good to hear. You know, this has been a common sentiment, I think a lot of folks are worried that they'll walk out the door and just be completely bereft, like totally bankrupt in minutes.

NK: You literally ... see the twenty-first century is all about taking money off of you in some way or another, and you're wanting to spend that because you're fucking miserable. Step outside of that and you realize that actually existence is pretty good. I have a very comfortable life. I'm blessed that I bought a house when it was great to buy a house and my house is now worth a shitload more money than what it was when I bought it. I've always had it in my back pocket; that was my safety blanket, that's my comfort blanket, but thankfully I've never had to cash it in.

MW: I'm kind of in the other direction. Like I'm in a postindustrial town in Pennsylvania, so the house that I'm sitting in is like worth maybe $80,000, but it won't ever appreciate until I'm a very old man ... if even then, it won't be worth much more than that. But it's so interesting because the value of an asset like a house is really quite relative when you live in it. You know, if this house were worth $1, the fact that I live in it is its value to me.

NK: That's the thing about that, part of the reason that drives me with this place is I don't want to do that, which is one of the reasons why I turned down all these big gigs and big jobs and stuff is because, no, I didn't want to leave this because it's a 200-year-old cottage that was an absolute shed when we bought it and we spent a lot of time restoring it back to its ... it's functional. You know what I mean? It's kind of, it's my hole and I have my man-cave, we've got a little garden in the countryside. It's great. So that's always been the ... "OK, you can always sell the house," but I don't want to sell the house.

MW: Yeah, I completely get it. So that's good to hear. When you left then, your primary source ... oh, you mentioned this before, but one of the questions I ask is, like, when you first left, what was your primary source of income?

NK: So I was made redundant in a way, the severance pay was really good. I think I walked away with ... I didn't have to work for about seven or eight months.

MW: OK. So it's a combo of savings, severance pay, and then freelancing that really kept you afloat.

NK: Yeah, but I was very quickly ready to go out and get some work. I gave myself two weeks holiday and then a month to get a job or I would go and be retrained to be a postman or something like that, because that was always the option that always … as long as I've got money there, it's like, OK, I could start on the bottom rung with a completely different career, but fuck it, I enjoy cooking. I'll just go be a cook … but I had that buffer zone always there.

But I got a job quite quickly and then that whole severance pay then became, "Hey, let's have an awesome holiday." The last couple of years have been tight at times and you do sometimes just have to sort of bite your tongue and do stuff you don't particularly want to do, but something else will come along.

MW: Yeah, absolutely. Okay, chapter three of this little interview has more questions about starting your new role. They don't probe the title, so that's fine. They're more about your day to day. So number one here is now that you're in a more indie role or a "nontraditional" one, you might say, a role other than with a big company working on a big product … what do your daily worries look like now?

NK: I'll think about that. That's a good one … When you're on a small-scale project, you've got do lots of things. Yeah. It's kind of that whole … well, the thing about AAA games is generally you're a specialist and if you're not a specialist, you're someone who has specialists to do his job for him. So it's about coordinating specialists. In indie games, in smaller-scale games, you're a generalist. You've got to turn your hand to everything. There's no one else to write design docs. There's no one else to maintain your website. There was no one else to write these really boring animation lists. There's no one else to rig this character. There's no one else to write this script. So my daily worries are not so much about the larger-scale stuff because as a designer I want to have my head in that space, but … the reason why our partnership works quite well is Alan very much is outward looking on the business side, and I am very myopic about the game. So there's an element of project management in there as well. As the designer, I'm the one that breaks down all the tasks, that writes the user stories, that task support, you know we've got the coders, we've got the artists, we got deals with all the sort of project management side of stuff, but at the same time, there's the game design documentation stuff and then all the shit that no one else wants to do. There's a constant stream of different things that need doing, and it's about maintaining the momentum in those tasks.

Because everything is really fucking important. So, it's all about triage. It's not about making the best thing, it's about doing it to a point where it works and it's kind of representative of what you want and then you move on to the next thing, and it's about building up your game slowly, rather than trying to obsess about one little detail because a game, again, games are greater than the sum of their parts, so it's about getting gameplay into your hands. It's determining—what are all the little steps to get this next bit of gameplay in my hands so I can play it and say, "no, that's shit" or "yeah, that's what we want more of." Whatever it needs to get that next playable iteration in whatever form it takes. Is that. Does that make sense? It's kind of weird.

MW: There's more varied things on your plate.

NK: Yes, but they all have the same ultimate objective ... So, my worry as design director of a small company is about the feel. Again, what is the feel of game? What am I doing? What are my verbs? Am I enjoying it? Is it fun? Is it interesting? So it's all about feeding back into that playable thing, that's all. You can always play it, you can always look at it, you can always feel it. Doesn't matter how many documents you write. It doesn't matter how many ideas you have or diagrams that you draw, the only thing that matters is the pad in your hand; that is your product. It's all well and good having grandiose spreadsheets and stuff like that, but it isn't your game, it's a fucking spreadsheet.

Yeah, so a lot of people really struggle to sort of visualize that on a real micro level. Everybody wants to think about ideas and game designs, they talk about ... "I've got a great idea for a game," but ideas are terrible, ideas are just this little blip bird that's a snapshot moment for the perfect distilled bit of a second of the game in your brain. It's not your game. You never chase ideas. You chase the thing in front of you, the video game, and you adapt your ideas to fit the game. You're shaping a piece of work ... again, it's a craft. You're building an object, only the object matters, much more than the nebulous shit in your head. And my colleagues hate me for this, because I'm very clear: "No, let's not worry about what the fucking camera is doing, let's not spend a week making this great transition. Let's assume it has a nice transition and focus on this shit." Because it's about building up an abstract picture of a game, but ignoring the stuff that that you know is going to come, the hygiene stuff. ... Hygiene being shit that you've got to do in a game, you always have to do it; nobody notices unless it's rubbish.

MW: We call it tech debt sometimes ... things like that ... like the loading screens, the texture mapping and power-of-twoing your, uh, your textures on objects and making sure animations repeat properly and yeah, I completely get it.

NK: So, I'm in the enviable position where all 1 have to worry about all day is what the game in front of me is doing ultimately. And while I may have spent that day doing some real micro-level tweaking of inputs, I may have written an animation list to send off to an animator, or I may have written a two-page brief for a concept artist, I may have done a little bit on the backstory. I may have started writing a PowerPoint deck to sell the game and also might have done a bit of brochure work, and I might have done a bit of just moving a camera around in the game. All of these things ultimately feed back into the product in your hand ... and you've just got to be able to make those crazy jumps all the time between all the different components. But you kind of have to do it in a fairly systematic fashion. We use a vaguely agile system. But it's just all about ... let's get all the tasks up on post-it notes on the wall and then shuffle them around. Right, you're doing that. OK. Off you go.

MW: The follow-up was, how is it different from your time in the mainstream games industry, but I think you've already kind of tied that in. I mean right in the opening. So when you talk about this kind of new role where you're sort of Jack-of-all-trades and have a whole wide variety... sort of a charcuterie board of tasks in front of you every day, is there an upside to that? Do you think that that works better for you? Do you feel better doing this than you did working on one very specific thing?

NK: I have the attention span of a goldfish, it's brilliant. I like the variety. I like the immersing myself in the game fully and every little thing is part of that. Being able to make those shifts of perspective from a real micro scale to a higher up thing, like ... how many levels have we got, what are those levels, what's the story, what's he doing, and then head back down to move that pixel around and then back out again. I enjoy doing it. I guess it's sort of ... it's great.

MW: To that end, you would say that this can't be a job for everybody, right?

NK: No, absolutely not, there are the people who I know who have been doing AAA stuff forever and will continue doing AAA stuff forever, and they fucking love it. You know, some really talented people in there, but they're happy just doing this one thing. I know guys who basically they spent their entire career building cars, it's what they do. They absolutely love building cars in 3D. They will always be building cars in 3D. Whereas that would just drive me insane.

MW: Yeah, exactly. So I think there's a personality match up, right? There exists somebody somewhere who is John Carmack–level brilliant at skeleton rigging in 3D models and that is what that guy or girl is going to do forever. And he or she loves it to death.

NK: And then you've got those whole alpha male or female psychopaths in this kind of corporate soup and they love what they're doing, and they're always going to carry on doing that thing because they're fucking psychopaths, but they love that whole mind games shit. Good for them. Great. They enjoy what they're doing. That's not for me.

MW: So all things considered, you'd make this move again then if you had all the cards equal.

NK: Yeah, it was the best thing to ever happen to me, quite honestly; I mean, the part I really enjoyed was being a game designer; by the time I went freelance, I had 20 years in the industry, and I think I'd had that moment where I thought, is this what I want to do? And actually realizing that yeah, being on the coal face, making stuff and having a bit more control … because, see, the other thing is I like a weird story, an interesting tale, I like an odd game, and that corporate environment is very, very conservative.

MW: Well, it's risk averse, right? There's a point where, and this isn't a finger-pointing thing … I mean there's a point where when you spend $200 million developing a game, you need to be able to absolutely guarantee your shareholders—in many cases of publicly traded companies anyway—you need to guarantee them that this thing's not going to be a flop, right?

NK: This is the thing … you can turn any stupid idea into a great game. Right?

So toward the end of my tenure at Sony, my job was to write concepts and get concepts greenlit, so this was not even "Let's dick around with a bit of code and do some prototypes," this was "We want to know exactly what our next big thing is." So it involved coming up with literally an endless succession of 10-page PowerPoint decks, raw game pitches with a bit of concept art, and that was about it. And then going up in front of literally 30 people in a room of executives and pitching your ideas.

If one person in that entire room of executives goes "Nah," that's it … and this was a room full of people who have that decision-making power—they know that they can say, "Yeah, brilliant, let's do it." But then if it all goes horribly wrong, they'll be the one who lost the company five, ten, fifteen, thirty million dollars, so no matter what, somebody in that room is going to say, "No we don't like that, don't do that." And after about … I think I went through about 18 pitches of just "Nah" … somebody in that room just didn't like that concept.

But now I'm in a different position. When we started Wushu, we basically sat down and said, "Right, what do you want to do?" You know, we have money here, we can spend some time doing this. What the fuck are we gonna do? And we literally, we have a list of about 12, we had a list of 12 concepts and they're all insanely different from shit involving dinosaurs and … let's see, there was Oliver Twist and there was some Viking shit and all kinds of variety, and everyone said, "We'll do this one, we'll do this and we kind of … "

Just being in a room of people who are positively inflated by that creative process, not just going "Nah, let's not do that because my career might go down the tube if we do." That was amazing. It's a really good feeling when everybody's sort of lifting it up, and as long as you've got that … but when you're in a corporate environment, they're relying on sales data from stuff that has gone well. The thought process is, "So we know this sells well," "We know this sold loads of copies," "So let's have more of those." But when you're trying to pitch interesting new stuff, not so much. Now, though, the room is like, "Well, this might be a winner, might be terrible idea, but let's give it a go nonetheless." It's very uplifting and you can genuinely do something interesting.

I think that the concept that we're working on right now has got some legs, but it's also got a certain commercial sense about it as well. Part of the design process is, "Who the fuck's gonna buy this?" We could think about those sorts of things, but not in those simple black-and-white terms that what an executive would do; he's got the numbers that say *Call of Duty* sold loads. So why the fuck not do whatever they did?

MW: Yeah, you're right. I mean everybody at the end of the day, even executives, you know, Linda has to make sure that when she goes home her paycheck is still there, and that her mortgage is still paid, and we all have those same stresses. So to some degree, it makes perfect sense that if you're responsible for something of that magnitude, where you don't have a lot of room to make mistakes. Yeah, I mean you'd be more conservative. Right?

Interesting. So two more totally wild-card questions and I think from the length of the interview, I think these are the worst kind for you. But it's fun. I like what's coming out of your mouth. So it's good. It's positive.

So … any words for folks who might be where you were? So you are a person who is sitting in an office, he's looking at the carpet wall and it's kind of like, you know what? Maybe this isn't. Maybe this isn't what I wanted when I got into games.

NK: Just do it. What've you got to lose? If you're as good as you think you are, but nobody else appreciates you, prove it. Prove it. Go out and be as good as you think you can be. There's always somebody who is willing to pay you money to do it. Admittedly, if you're shit and you think you're good and you go out and fail, well then go do something else. Clearly you're not made out to be in this career, but don't sit and worry about it. It's just a bit of a bullshit "follow your dreams" sort of thing, but it's a bit more pragmatic than that. It's like, do you want make games? Are you good at making games? Can you make a career out of games? If not, go do something else that you actually enjoy, because there's plenty of things out there that you could do for the money that can get you through life.

Games can be a terrible, cruel, merciless industry. It has the potential of completely breaking you and you need to realize, you are the means of production. You are the capital, so go find work elsewhere if you need to.

MW: Last wild card and this one is ... anything at all you'd like to add? Anything.

NK: Oh, shit ... making games is really good. Making games is interesting and weird and constantly surprises me, but it's also really hard and frustrating. It's way harder than what you think it is. A lot of people don't get how hard making games is. So even just making a game, just finishing it and getting it to market. Even if it was just terrible. Some licensed show jumping simulator. I've done *Wheel of Fortune* games and *Family Fortunes* games in the past. By making a game, even if this is a game you don't particularly want to make, will teach you more about making games, and will make sure that the game you make eventually is going to be better. You're learning it while you're making. You're constantly learning, you're constantly reinventing the wheel. You're constantly thinking of how to do things in a new and interesting way ... and that's kind of cool, regardless of what it is you're actually making.

MW: That's been super. Thanks again, Nigel, it's been awesome and I'm going to stop the recording whenever ... of course we can still chat for a minute, but thanks so much.

NK: I do have a tendency to ramble about this.

Nobody would pretend that an entrepreneurial spirit doesn't also come with a problem with rigidity and arbitrary authority. Entrepreneurs are often seen as "disruptors," and indies are the games industry's turtleneck-wearing startup superstars. Nigel felt the rigid and controlled environment and its cold corporate grasp were stifling his creativity, and found happiness when he was able to be most creative. Now, like so many individuals in other industries, he's running his own business, but most importantly, he's making games.

Morgan Kennedy, formerly Ubisoft

Morgan and I currently work together at Player Research, a user research and analytics consulting firm owned by Keywords Studios. I met Morgan when he left Ubisoft to join our team in Montreal. Morgan has had a more nontraditional entry into the industry, working as a cook on a ship, then working in an academic capacity, before eventually working indie, AAA, and finally contracting. His nonstandard path has given him a unique perspective, and I think the most positive of my interviewees.

Still, common threads bind Morgan's experience to other folks. If you read carefully, some of them will jump out at you.

MW: Hey Morgan—thanks for taking the interview. So the very first question is simple: please introduce yourself and tell me a little bit about your work in games.

MK: OK—Hi, my name is Morgan Kennedy. I am studio lead and senior user researcher at Player Research in Montreal. I've been doing games usability research since 2010. I worked at Ubisoft for ... I think four years and 11 months, almost five years, and I worked on four and a half *Assassin's Creed* titles during that time.

MW: ... Four and a half?

MK: Well, half so ... I think the first title that I worked on was *Revelations*, and the last one that's got my name in the credits is *Unity*, actually.

MW: OK, so four and a half, I see. I didn't understand there at first, but that makes sense.

MK: Yeah, I just worked on the multiplayer for *Revelations*, briefly.

MW: All right, give me one hot second to pull up a list of questions ... OK. Next one. There are a few questions here about your life in games generally. If you need to omit anything that's covered in an NDA or you just don't want to talk about, you can go ahead and do that and I won't bug you about it.

So that's pretty much that. I got you to answer already the "How long have you been working in games slash give me a career rundown." So next bit is a little more emotional squishy. Can you describe to me when you first knew you wanted to work in video games?

MK: Yeah, actually, I grew up in rural Vermont and I remember playing *Prince of Persia* and turning the box over and seeing that it was made at Ubisoft, Montreal. And I realized it's like—hey, wait a minute, that's like two and half hours from here, that's a place I can go to where they make video games. So actually that was my goal was to work with the *Prince of Persia* team, yeah, to work on the *Prince of Persia* franchise or work with that team. It was sort of my childhood dream fulfilled when I started doing usability and play testing for *Assassin's Creed*.

MW: Oh, that's funny. So *Prince of Persia*, you mean the original, more like Sega or Super Nintendo or whatever one?

MK: Oh no, no, I mean the PS2 one.

MW: Oh, sorry, yeah, I guess that makes more sense with the timeline.

MK: Yeah, exactly.

MW: Cool. OK. You sort of already mentioned this, but what was the transition like? How did you get into the games industry? Everyone always talks about "breaking into the games industry." What was that moment for you? Was it just the direct apply, get hired, or was there some in between?

MK: Yeah, I actually was working at Concordia University where I was coordinating and running an academic games research lab. I'd finished a graduate certificate in interaction design and got hired as the coordinator for a new lab that was devoted to video games specifically. So while I was the coordinator there, I actually took my week's paid vacation and volunteered as a play tester for *Assassin's Creed: Brotherhood*. So I sat in an air conditioned room at Ubisoft and played *Assassin's Creed* for a week for my vacation. And I think it was the second day I was there, one of the moderators actually asked me what I did, we were just speaking casually. I said—Oh, I'm a coordinator for this new lab at Concordia, and at the time we were doing ethnographic research on players of the Nintendo Wii, coordinating those studies, and he basically said, bring me your CV tomorrow; we're actually hiring for that role right now.

MW: Oh wow.

MK: I think everyone that's been in the game industry for a little while knows the experience where like people's job titles can be wildly different even if they're doing the same role. But like the literal title was "research coordinator" at the university and the title that they were hiring for—what analysts were called at the time—was like "playtest coordinator," or "user research coordinator." So actually, the titles matched and the work was similar obviously, too. But they essentially were like, OK, we're interested in you coming in for interviews. So I went through the interview process. I was the only … I was the first sort of pure anglophone that they hired in the lab. So I was not from Canada, not from Montreal, and French isn't my native language. So I don't know if that's why, but it went through like three or four interviews before I was actually hired.

MW: OK. So I know that now you work for a consultancy firm and between now and at Ubisoft, you also worked on an indie title. Can you tell me a little bit about that?

MK: Yeah. I worked at Ubisoft in 2015, I think, then left to do an interdisciplinary master's degree, again at Concordia. And during that time I'd been working as a consultant just on my own for smaller indie companies, some of the companies in Montreal, and I was actually hired by Compulsion Games as their user research manager while I was in the midst of doing this master's degree. I actually did that up until I was hired, essentially, with a small gap where I was in Japan right up until I was hired by Player Research.

MW: Oh, OK. So most of the respondents in the book so far, not all of them, but most of them had a pretty negative experience working AAA. So one of the reasons I was really interested in speaking with you is because I don't think everyone that leaves AAA has a horrific nightmare experience. I think there are some people that see something in indie they want to do or something in consultancy or freelancing that they want to do and they make that change on completely good terms.

I'm trying to address everybody with this book ... everybody that's sitting in a AAA studio that might want to move out of that role, whether that be just because they want to advance their career or because they really hate it, you know, it depends on the person, obviously, but I want to show them that there are people out there that are working in games, possibly at companies they've never heard of, making a great living, and that that's completely possible for them to do.

So, I guess one of the things I'll addresses is—this definitely does not have to be sneery or finger-pointing, to be clear—what are some of the things that made you want to move away from Ubisoft and move into a new career?

MK: Well, I actually have a very specific ... I mean my answer I think is going to be really different from the other folks you've spoken to.

MW: Oh, and that's totally fine. Again, I'm trying to get a wide rather than a deep narrative here, if that makes sense?

MK: Yep. So, actually, I'm going to have to tell a story in order to ...

MW: That's OK, tell a story, by all means!

MK: Well, since I arrived in Montreal in 2008, I'd been involved in a research project through Concordia led by my thesis adviser and professor, Professor Jason Lewis and his partner Skawennati, who is Mohawk and from Kahnawake reserve, which is the Mohawk reserve just south of Montreal. And the project was to teach Mohawk students, teenagers, really, in Kahnawake schools how to make video games that were based on traditional Mohawk stories. So, it's something I've been involved with for the past 10 years. It was one of the first groups I joined when I came to Montreal.

MW: This reminds me a lot of that *Never Alone* project.

MK: Yeah. Actually, yeah. The difference between that game and the games from this project are that the students, like, literally make them.

MW: Oh, OK.

MK: So we're not like ... *Never Alone*, by my understanding, was developed by Eli Media in conjunction with and funded by Cook County Tribal Council in Alaska. It wasn't the case that the Cook County tribal members were actually directly involved in the development of the game. In this case, we actually would recruit industry professionals to come to the reserve to go to Kahnawake school and lead workshops on 3D animation, game design, production, management, and then the students themselves would choose roles. And then over the course of 10 weeks, or a summer, or sometimes a couple of years on one of the projects, actually develop games that are based on their own culture, essentially.

MW: Interesting. I may follow up with you with a forwarding email to just spell out these things for me because I want to make sure I get the spelling correct and cite everyone correctly. So just that's a side note, but please carry on.

MK: Yeah, for sure. So, that was something I'd been doing continuously, actually, I mean, I'm still involved on some level. Shortly after I joined Ubisoft, I learned that there was a game in production in the *Assassin's Creed* series that actually featured a Mohawk protagonist. And of course that game is *Assassin's Creed III*. And so as sort of quickly as I could, I aimed for the role of the person doing play tests for that project, because I wanted to be involved for obvious reasons. So that sort of became my focus for really like about half of the time I was there when they started ... probably from when the game was in alpha up to when we were doing actual play tests with participants from outside the studio and then once it shipped, working on the DLC.

So for me, it was this rare moment where all of a sudden my personal interests or ... sort of my academic interests, where my nonwork interests and my work interests all of a sudden were perfectly aligned. I recruited people from the *Assassin's Creed* team to come to the reserve and actually teach these actual Mohawk students. And Mohawk students came to Ubisoft to play test the game and give comments on it.

MW: I think that sounds like a wonderful opportunity.

MK: Yeah. And to be honest ... And there were many, many people involved in a game like *Assassin's Creed* and there were also many people involved in terms of ensuring that the cultural content of the game—as in the Mohawk content—was like ... it's still science fiction, obviously, but it was, you know, respectful and well done and authentic. There's obviously a lot of potential for something like that to be done badly.

And again, a lot of these things were outside of my job description. I was a playtest analyst for the project, but in terms of the things that I was doing that were most meaningful to me, it was like recruiting people that were very intimately associated with the game, *Assassin's Creed III* ... to come to the reserve to actually meet and work with Mohawk students who were also making video games about themselves. I think it just created this really nice positive feedback loop between those two groups. In addition to, of course, all the other work that was being done officially. They hired Thomas Deer, a consultant who's actually familiar with Mohawk culture, who's Mohawk, I think he's Mohawk. I should confirm that. And anyway, all of the work that was being done to ensure that the historical parts of *ACIII* were correct and culturally respectful.

In addition to that, being able to help create this direct connection with the people that are working on a game and the people who are being depicted in the game on some level was ... well to be honest, it was like I couldn't have hoped or anticipated something like that would have happened in my career. And to be honest, the reason why I left Ubisoft shortly after that, a year and a half or two years after that was because I just realized that the chances of that … It was like sort of like two lightning bolts striking the ground in the same place, that was highly unlikely to happen again in the same job, you know?

So that was actually the reason why I decided it was time to move on. It wasn't because of … It was "mission accomplished" is sort of the wrong metaphor, but I just recognized that what just happened was extremely unique and unlikely to happen again in the same context.

MW: So this was a career advancement move in that sense?

MK: No, it was like a life moment where I was still sort of reeling, and again, I don't know how useful this will be, but like it was one of those moments where I thought … OK, I looked back and I thought, I grew up two and a half hours from here in rural Vermont and wanted to work with the *Prince of Persia* team. That was like a childhood dream. I fulfilled that dream. And then to be able to also work with people from a Mohawk reserve, make that connection between the studio and the reserve in like an informal way, in an unofficial way while working on this thing. It's just like, that's so much positive coincidence that it was just like a life thing. It's like, OK, I need to figure out what the next two lightning bolts are going to be because lightning just doesn't strike three times.

MW: I understand.

MK: Does that make sense?

MW: No, no, it does. So I guess, then, the thing I'd like to tease out is what then piqued your interest to start working on *We Happy Few*?

MK: Yeah, I'd met people from Compulsion, actually, Whitney, the art director from Compulsion, is also from Vermont. We grew up like 30 minutes away from each other, although we didn't know each other as kids or anything.

MW: I think that's pretty much Vermont.

MK: Yeah, exactly.

MW: Yeah, yeah.

MK: Yeah, and so I was aware of that project. I met the team and I really, really, really liked them. I really like the game, actually, to be honest. I mean I was playing it and ... I guess without going into anything that would be covered by an NDA ... to be honest, I don't know if I ever signed an NDA with them. I don't know if they required [them] at this studio when I joined.

MW: Indies are often pretty loose, I mean the projects I work on now, we don't have NDAs, you know.

MK: Yeah. I mean, to be honest, I think I had to convince Guillaume— the studio head—that we should have people who playtest the game sign NDAs. I think the first time I asked him, his reaction was like ... I think he literally said—"I don't give a shit, it's frickin' free advertising for us."

MW: That's funny. Yeah. Sorry, carry on.

MK: So the way I met them is after leaving Ubisoft I had friends that were working at Minority Media, which made *Papo &. Yo* for the PlayStation 3, which is another kind of like "III" indie studio; it was started by Vander Caballero from EA. So through them I met some ... I think after leaving Ubisoft I did a little bit of consulting for them, too ... I can't remember. Anyway, then through them I met the people at Compulsion and they were looking for similar things; they were a small studio. They didn't really have the ability to do usability or UX research. So yeah, I just met them ... No, sorry, wait ... this is an even longer story.

MW: It's OK.

MK: While I was at Concordia, I was involved in this high-minded but ultimately unsuccessful project to see if it was possible to create a console that would connect libraries to indie developers. It was basically like an indie-focused ... It was really just preliminary research trying to determine if it would be possible to create an actual hardware device that could both meet the needs of libraries and also be a home for indie video games. So as part of that, I actually did a bunch of interviews with indie developers in Montreal about what their needs were, essentially for that, or like how they made money. Like, essentially how that could possibly fit into their strategy for their overall business and for making the kinds of games that they were making. Through that, that's how actually, I think, I first had a conversation with Guillaume and Sam at Compulsion.

MW: OK, cool. So it sounds to me like through the conversations you're having that … if this would be a fair assessment, that you are kind of a challenge seeker, or a creative experience seeker. So there's a few people in the games industry that have … in … not so nice words equated … That I've spoken to so far, that have said they grew unhappy with their role because at some point they went from making games at a holistic level to making, say, tires in a racing game all day and nothing else.

MK: Making pizza.

MW: Correct. Or something very specific. So they went from broadly being the AI programmer on all AI on a game all the way down to like: now I am the very specific combat and pathfinding AI programmer. Then eventually their role became so laser focused and specialized that they just left because they wanted a more general challenge. They're not—at least the folks I've spoken to so far—vitriolic about that. They're not saying things like, "fuck my old company for putting me in this very specialized role" per se, but they are sharing that the roles just didn't fulfill the need to create anymore. It didn't scratch the itch, so to speak.

MK: Yeah. I mean, for better or worse, the AAA game industry is looking for specialists. That's essentially the way that the studios are structured. So it's inevitable, I guess, it's inevitable that you sort of end up becoming very, very specialized. Like all I did was *Assassin's Creed*, not all, but the majority of my time was doing *Assassin's Creed* play tests. And I think there was one year, to be honest, where I think I literally cut and pasted my Outlook calendar for one year to the other—not in terms of individual meetings, obviously—but in terms of like milestones and stuff like that. I think that was the moment, it was like, OK this has been a good experience, but maybe it's time to think about something else.

MW: Well, yeah … and so that's not necessarily inherently negative, that's the one thing I want to tease out here is that people leave careers for all kinds of reasons; some of them are positive, like "I got a better offer elsewhere." Some of them are kind of just neutral, like "this wasn't doing it for me anymore," like what you seem to be saying. And some of them are very negative, like "I was being worked to death." There's all ends of the spectrum in this book so far. So I think you fit somewhere.

MK: Certainly the answer, then, is that I knew … I felt like after five years on *Assassin's Creed*, I knew what my life would be like if I kept working in the current role on the project I was on and it was fine, it's a good life. I'm not complaining. But I just realized I wanted to do something different.

MW: Yeah, I get you. So I guess there's a "how do you do it" question that I think a lot of people have. Many people that are in the same situation you were in, even if it's just—ah, "I don't really want to be doing the same thing all the time," or whatever. You know, again, not trying to be negative, but they're looking for something new.

But I think there's a bit of a fear in the industry that if you start actively looking for new opportunities, this is still a pretty small industry, so word gets around pretty quickly. So do you have to sneak around a bit, and that feels dishonest and casts a cloud over the whole thing. The other option, of course, is to just straight-up quit and go look for a job. But of course that terrifies people because of the financial realities of that and whatnot.

So I guess if you could describe a little bit of how you went about seeking a new venture without burning a bridge, I think that'd be an interesting angle?

MK: Yeah, sure … and again, this may or may not be useful to anyone else because, what actually happened is that I'd actually applied and gotten into this interdisciplinary master's program and immediately gotten hired at Ubisoft. So I said OK, and I had to essentially put that master's degree on hold. I didn't even enroll, I actually postponed enrollment for … well, actually, to be honest, long enough that they kicked me out of the program and made me reapply when I did finally go. So, I think I postponed three years in a row and they said if you postpone it any longer then you have to reapply and so then I reapplied and that was year five at Ubisoft. So I essentially just went back to the school that I had originally been planning to go to in the first place.

MW: So you sort of had an escape route?

MK: Yeah. And actually, maybe that's the lesson, is that, most … Maybe it's not the case now, but when I joined … Yeah, and actually, this is something I would tell students, counterintuitively, but it's important … if you get a job in the video game industry … When I was getting a job at the video game industry, I think the average lifespan of a developer was five years.

MW: Yeah. It's probably about the same now, to be honest. I don't have data on that on hand, but the turnover is brutal.

MK: Yeah, so if you are getting a job in the video game industry, you should essentially already have your exit strategy if you know that in five years, statistically, you'll likely no longer be working in that industry. And so that was my exit strategy, to go and do this degree, which I'd been putting off for five years, essentially. Also, the project that I just explained at the beginning had just received funding from the Canadian government for a couple of million dollars, which is not a lot in video games, but …

MW: A ton for an academic, yes.

MK: Yeah. So it was just like perfect timing. For a while I was actually working, I don't remember what, three-quarters time or something like that at Ubisoft so I could go to my classes, which were mostly at night. Then I would take my vacation time at the end of each semester to write my papers, essentially. So for a brief moment I was actually going to school full time and working full time, which honestly was fun, but clearly not sustainable. So essentially, I asked to go on leave for three months. They said yes and I came back from leave and worked some more and said, OK I'm going to pursue this school thing because my professor just got funding, essentially.

MW: Got it. So your new venture, what you're doing now, obviously explaining it to me is a little bit bizarre since we work together, but can you tell me a little bit about what you do now and how that's kind of scratching the itch that you've talked about for the sake of those reading?

MK: Yeah, well, actually, I essentially built the user research department at Compulsion from the ground up. It was only me doing it and a couple of QA testers who I sometimes sort of drafted to help me with tests. But what I realized when I spoke to Graham [McAllister at Player Research], what I said initially is that I really missed that feeling of being at the beginning of a new thing, like starting a new lab. Because I helped start a lab at Concordia called Techniculture Art and Games. I worked in that lab that I spoke of that my professor runs that taught the workshops on the reserve at Kahnawake. I also randomly worked at a Cornell research lab during the summers doing, like an offshore marine sciences lab, which I don't actually have any expertise in, but it was just fun.

So, I realized I missed that feeling of starting something new, like starting a new venture, essentially. So it seemed like a perfect fit. I was actually at this point at the end of my master's degree. I finished my classes, met Graham at a conference, I guess now two years ago, and he just said that they were looking for someone to open a new lab here in Montreal, asked if I was interested; I said definitely. Because it's nice to have total ownership over something, like doing everything from like screwing together the furniture to actually running the business, I was looking for that kind of opportunity.

MW: That's sort of the startup feeling that a lot of people seem to like.

MK: Exactly.

MW: And that's kind of … I think that's present in a lot of indie games, right? I feel like an indie game developer at one moment is an AI programmer, at the next moment is a plumber, at the next moment is a salesperson. So I think that flexibility, I think a lot of people, especially academics, do talk about that a lot, that they grow very bored if they don't have a wide variety of challenges.

I mean, this was a common topic back when I taught as well. One of the things that academics would say they really enjoyed about their job was like, well you're paid pretty poorly and blah, blah, blah, but you have all of these very interesting new challenges that are directly related to what you're interested in.

MK: Yeah, exactly.

MW: That's kind of fortuitous in your case. You really did kind of bounce from interesting thing, to interesting thing, to interesting thing. So that's positive.

MK: This isn't just something I'm saying to seem humble. I just feel really, really lucky that I've gotten to work with the people that I've gotten to work with and on the projects that I have.

MW: That's cool. I think it does add a lot of flavor ...

MK: ... and I think there's an incredible amount of luck involved in that kind of thing that's pretty unacknowledged by people when they're giving advice about how to succeed in your career. Preparation and all that stuff is important, but a lot of it is luck.

MW: There is certain amount of serendipity, for sure. I used to tell my students, speak to everyone who is taking the time to speak to you. Because it's so bizarre which human being you happen to bump into will be your next boss or whatever.

MK: Exactly. Exactly.

MW: So, what's the daily struggle now look like? So this is a more nontraditional games role, right? Like you're in the games industry but you're not a AAA developer in a traditional studio ... When someone asks you, "Oh you work in video games?", it's not like, "Oh, I make *Call of Duty*," or you're not specifically tied to a project or a studio like you were previously. What do the day's challenges look like now as compared to when you were in AAA?

MK: That's a good question. I guess the challenge is the thing that I also enjoy. But when you're starting a new lab, a new anything, really, there's a nearly infinite number of tasks that need to be done, requiring a very, very wide range of skills. So it's essentially managing that, just keeping all the balls in the air, I guess, you know. That's the biggest challenge.

MW: So you had a more predictable schedule when you were in AAA, then. You did say you literally copy and pasted your Outlook calendar year-over-year.

MK: Yeah, exactly.

MW: So do you feel like that's a better fit for you?

MK: Yeah, it's better for me. I think there are people that would be very well served by working in AAA. Which is not to say that I was not, or that I would not like to go back. I mean, to be honest, my post-master's plan was to start applying for jobs at other, maybe not AAA game studios, but other publishers, even some nongame stuff. When I was making my first round of job applications, Spotify was hiring a senior user researcher, Soundcloud was hiring a senior user researcher. They're both based in Berlin. I lived in Berlin, so that was option two, was to apply to those jobs and consider moving back there.

MW: Oh, interesting.

MK: So when I was in Japan, I got a grant from the Japanese government to go there for four months and interview and study Japanese game developers regarding how they use narrative in their games. So I met a professor at Ritsumeikan University, and so in the back of my mind it was like, "Yeah, I want to do a PhD in Japan." That was the other backup plan, I guess.

MW: You definitely sound like you have a lot of balls in the air.

MK: Yeah, I guess. There's just so many interesting things in the world that you could literally spend your entire life studying them and never run out of things to do. That's how I feel.

MW: So I think you kind of jumped my next question, which was, if you had the opportunity at a big AAA entity that wanted you back, and I don't mean quit your current job, whatever, but I mean in the distant future, could you see yourself working at a AAA studio again?

MK: Yeah, sure. I mean the determining factor isn't like AAA or not AAA. it's more like cultural and business model fit. You know what I mean?

MW: Yeah, I completely understand.

MK: And to be honest, and this is sort of weirdly personal as well, but when I left Compulsion, and when you leave a company, there are exit interviews that they often do as a formality, but Guillaume, the studio head, really took the time and sat me down for probably over an hour, actually. He really talked through what he felt I contributed to the team, to the studio, and then gave me very, very specific recommendations, because he's also been in the game industry for a very long time. So he actually gave very specific recommendations in terms of lists of studios that he thought I would really enjoy working at, and really enjoy generally, ones that would be a really good fit based on my personality and areas of expertise and the culture of the studio.

So I won't say the specific names because that might be sort of awkward, but I really appreciated that. And one of the things out of that conversation, one of the things I was looking for was some place that had more of a flat hierarchy than Ubisoft, which is known for being a more hierarchical studio, I guess. Player Research was a great fit for that.

MW: That's been interesting. You know, it seems like you've really run into kind of the "good guy Gregs" of the industry, honestly. Because as you say, my exit interview from Sony was, it was a formality. I spoke to an HR person that I'd never met before, she was in an office that I had never been to before. She had no idea who I was. I had no idea who she was. And she blandly read off a series of perfunctory questions that I answered with an equal degree of pallor and that was that. So no, that's really interesting and I love to see …

MK: … [laughs], yeah I've had a lot of different jobs so I've had all of those kind of experiences too, I'm just telling you about the good ones.

MW: Sure. I have two short wild-card questions, and then we're done. Any words for folks who might be where you were before you changed? And this can be literally anything. So if you're a person who is sitting and is kind of thinking—"hm, I think it's time for the next thing," and that's sort of eating at you in the back of your mind. Do you have anything that you would say to that Morgan?

MK: Yeah. Well, I guess the real trick is to develop your instincts to the point you can trust them and then trust your instincts.

MW: OK. I understand.

MK: Or in other words, don't be scared. Because, honestly, I think I tried … I think this is fine for me to say. I think I tried three different times to give my notice at Ubisoft … as in like, I booked a meeting with my immediate supervisor, went into the meeting room intending to give notice and chickened out.

MW: Yeah. That's come up a few times, actually.

MK: Yeah, and then had to come up with some other justification why I wanted to meet with them and even the third time … Because it's a bit like the, what do they call it? Like the golden handcuffs, you know, it's a great job, your dream job from when you were a kid and you're being paid well and most companies provide good benefits and that kind of thing. Like you have that dream job, it's very, very hard to leave it for something that's unknown, you know?

MW: Now that conversation has actually come up a few times. So you did hit on something interesting that other people have definitely mentioned, which is that you feel almost ungrateful. Like, "I've gotten so far in this thing that everyone wants to be in and now I'm leaving. What is wrong with me?" Like, there's this guilty feeling keeping you there—that conversation has come up more than once.

I have also, on the other hand, heard people express a feeling that companies have weaponized that "dream job" narrative so that they don't leave, sort of more a negative interpretation. Rather than being more positive and personal about it, like yourself.

MK: I'm a pretty open person. So when I would speak to strangers, or just in casual conversation, and I would tell them that I just left Ubisoft or I was leaving Ubisoft, they all were like, "You're crazy." The reaction on their faces was like you're making a terrible, terrible mistake … You know what I mean? These were people I didn't know well, so it's not like I necessarily took the advice … or the implied advice to heart or anything. But that was true, if you tell a stranger—"Hey, I'm leaving this well-paid dream job, working for a video game company," you sound absolutely crazy.

MW: Last wild-card question. Anything at all you want to add? And depending on what it is, we'll slap it in the book. Literally anything.

MK: Yes. Don't be limited by your own sense of what is possible, because truthfully, when I graduated from Concordia with my graduate certificate in interaction design, I applied to a whole bunch of things … I did video game studios in Montreal for a variety of reasons; none of those jobs worked out. I actually moved back to the States and took a job managing a restaurant. And the conclusion I came to at that moment was, "Well, I guess sometimes things just don't work out in life." Which was exactly the wrong conclusion because now I'm sitting here telling you the story of having worked at Ubisoft Montreal for five years and now leading the studio at Player Research. All of which in retrospect seems inevitable, right? But the actual life lesson that I sort of told myself I had just learned was like, "Sometimes things don't work out," but they do, in fact.

MW: I admire your general level of positivity and hopefulness. Thanks again for the interview, it's been great.

Certainly a more positive outlook; Morgan left for career advancement and to find a new challenge. The important anchor here is that the reason for leaving, breaking out, making a change need not be negative. Maybe moving out of AAA is just the next interesting challenge in your already very interesting career.

I hope the above interviews have given you some insight. It's easy to assume, with the games industry's very public struggles, that those who leave do so in order to escape. As you can see, however, many of the folks in this book and, indeed, many folks across the planet are leaving on positive terms, even career-advancing terms, to seek new opportunities. There is a flourishing scene of independent developers, freelancers, contracting firms, and more available to you if you happen to be of even the slightest entrepreneurial persuasion.

Of course, there are the ugly stories as well. Ben nearly died, Nigel grew dead on the inside, and both made their escape as quickly as they could manage it thereafter. It's been my intention with these interviews to show you that the reasons people are leaving are as varied as the people themselves—but make no mistake, they *are* leaving. As part of a larger exodus out of city centers happening across the United States and the globe, people are slowly decentralizing the games industry. There are all kinds of factors playing into this, between unionization efforts, crunch and work conditions, the proliferation of remote work currently happening across all industries, and reaction to cost of living in city centers.

Perhaps in 10 years, we'll have indie games like we have craft beer, where every small- to medium-sized town across America has a thriving development scene providing good, family-sustaining jobs to developers. Two decades ago, nobody could have predicted the proliferation of small-town craft breweries in the face of almighty Anheuser, but here we are.

how do I do it?

This chapter is designed to address a few of the most common trepidations about leaving the games industry, and indeed leaving your job generally.

As the interviewees addressed, that first step is a doozy. Nobody wants to walk into their immediate supervisor's office and tell them that they're done. It's scary, often confrontational, and almost never a pleasant experience. Like most things, though, the real trouble can sometimes start after you've made the change. Freelancing and contracting are great, but it's a huge amount of work to secure what was previously a predictable paycheck—layoffs notwithstanding.

how do I get money, though?

Understandably, the first thing many professionals worry about when making a move out of a stable job, no matter how distasteful it may have become, is where their next paycheck is coming from.

This section will deal with how to make sure you have enough money to continue your life. One of the biggest challenges I had to face when entering into an entrepreneurial situation was being brutally honest with myself about where my money was going. When I was young, my mother would carry around a little notebook and write down every penny that came in and out. This seemed insane to me as a teenager, but we were not wealthy, and she somehow managed to make it all work.

While I'm not saying you need to log every penny, you will have to be honest about your spending habits. How much do you spend on new clothing? Drinks? Dining out? Subscriptions to things you don't use? ... and so on. I personally shaved off about $300 each month without even noticing a difference this way, and while that doesn't sound like much right now, read on.

Save Some Cash

The single most important source of capital for leaving your current employment to seek greener pastures is your current employment, period. While you may feel dishonest continuing to collect a paycheck while you know you are actively looking elsewhere, I invite you to cast those moral trepidations aside and simply make sure you're still doing your best work nine-to-five ... or eight-to-eight, as the case may be, every single day. By giving your absolute best to your job, you gain a few major benefits:

- The company will be more likely to look favorably upon you, even when you leave, for all the value you've added.
- You'll likely leave without burning any bridges. Your employer will be significantly more upset if they realize you've been phoning it in for a month.
- When you get home from work, you can feel good about preparing for your new adventure.

Most wealth and investment books advise that you can immediately deposit up to 10% of your paycheck directly into an interest-yielding investment or savings account without noticing a significant difference in your quality of life. Mind you, most of those books were written by baby boomers with spare cash and without a quarter-million-dollar student loan. Regardless, there is some truth here. By chopping off 10% of your paycheck and immediately storing it into a fund entirely dedicated to making a career change, you can establish a cushion in a relatively short amount of time.

I'm certainly not saying you have to *stop* at 10%; rather, I'm suggesting that it makes a great starting point. If you're anything like me, your paydays probably look something like this: you get your paycheck, then around noon, or whenever you get a spare second, you go through and pay all of your mandatory bills like mortgage, utilities, and so on. After that, you pay down credit cards that you've been using for your discretionary spending for the last two weeks. If you're lucky, you even pay them down to zero. Any leftover cash can then be invested into the same, which brings me to …

Trim the Fat

It seems like the new economy for startups is incremental payments. "Box" shipments of random crap sent to you once a month are all the rage, often at a savage markup. Food subscription services that replaced going to a market and buying food like a normal human being charge upwards of $150 per *week* to feed your family. You probably also have five or six streaming services you don't use, auto-renewal subscriptions and offers you've never canceled, bills on auto-withdraw that you don't monitor, and sneaky fees and interest. We've become so used to things like Amazon Prime, Netflix, and our monthly Ferret Food Box being automatically thrown on the debt pile that we've become totally unfamiliar with the concept of being overcharged. Nobody has to look you in the eye to gouge you anymore.

Another more uncomfortable place to be honest with yourself is your personal spending. Nigel, Ben, and I all expressed the same opinion in our stories: *when you are unhappy at work, you will spend irresponsibly outside of work to try to compensate.* Looking back at my spending history, during my time at PlayStation, I was spending an average of $450 a month on alcohol, $550 on restaurants, and $500 on entertainment (movie and concert tickets, events, etc.) That's $1500 a month, enough to support a considerable mortgage in most parts of the world. This is not to say that you shouldn't eat, drink, and be merry. I will wager, however, that if you're reading this book and are unhappy with your current situation at work, you'll find considerable bloat in your "try to make myself happy" budget.

This says nothing, of course, about more traditional "thrifty" techniques you can use to save or gather up money, like revolving 0% credit cards, switching phone or utility companies, coupons, and that sort of thing, though those are mostly outside of the scope of this book. However, this all leads me to one major point—if you're serious about making a massive life change …

Consider Your Location

As of the time of writing, a modest 1300-square-foot single-family home in Palo Alto, California, is $1,998,000, representing a monthly mortgage cost of roughly $8300. A similar modest two-bedroom

1300-square-foot single-family home in Erie, Pennsylvania, costs $64,990, representing a monthly mortgage cost of $284, *literally 30 times less*. While I'm not suggesting you move to Erie (but maybe do; it's really nice here), my larger point is this: you keep yourself busy doing the same activities wherever you live.

In California, my wife and I enjoyed going to the beach, seeing a baseball game, going to the movies, going on microbrewery and winery tours, and relaxing at home with friends and some video games. In Erie, we enjoy going to the beach, seeing a baseball game, going to the movies ... you get the idea. The fundamental difference is that I'm paying less for my mortgage here than I did to park my car in California, with no commute.

The more important point is the salary you have to command in order to maintain your quality of life. A singular issue I run into when discussing leaving the industry proper with other developers is the contention that they have to maintain exactly the same salary or higher, or they will be unable to maintain a happy, healthy quality of life. If there existed a magic wand I could use to shake a belief from people's minds, I would use it on these people and flat-earthers.

As you leave the metropolis, the cost of absolutely everything decreases. Gasoline, beer, groceries, taxes, land, property, utilities, and more all plummet. When leaving, I personally took a massive, five-digit pay cut to take my remote job, but now save more than four times the amount of money per month I did when working in California. How is this possible? If we use the above mortgage numbers as a baseline, and *ignore all other costs besides housing*—a person in Palo Alto would require a minimum yearly income of $99,600 to an Erieite's $3408 to maintain the same home. If you're serious about moving into an entrepreneurial role, it may be time to consider a move. There's also a way you can make a California salary in Idaho ...

Remote Work

There's a pretty good chance you're a skilled game developer if you're reading a book titled *Breaking Out of the Games Industry*. If that's the case, I'm pleased to announce that, like most industries, the games industry is slowly coming around to the idea of 100% telecommute.

We've seen a remote boom around the country in the last few years. There are a few things to be said about it. First, there's intrinsic value to being in your home—if I can do my job in my living room without pants versus in an office in a collared shirt, that's valuable.

Additionally, working from the house confers certain monetary benefits. Children can be cared for by the worker at home, eschewing child-care costs. Working from home reduces automobile, insurance, gas, parking, and other commute-related costs. People who work from home have resources available that prevent them from eating out, going for coffee midday, or punching down three cocktails at happy hour with the office crew. There are money and quality of life savings all around.

There are downsides, of course. Only certain companies are comfortable with the idea of an employee being 100% remote, particularly if you are dealing with sensitive or confidential information. Additionally, certain roles do not work well remotely. HR, production, or other roles that require daily, face-to-face interaction with members of the team are especially hard to telecommute. If you work in a technical, IT, or asset production role, the likelihood of you being able to telecommute increases. In the games industry, remote willingness seems to also depend on production phase. If your company is in hard crank on a project trying to get to content complete, so long as you're banging out assets, clearing the backlog, and the burn chart is going down, your immediate supervisor probably doesn't care where you're doing it. Your mileage may vary, and it will be interesting to see how this plays out in the next few years.

If your job can't go 100% telecommute, you probably need to quit. If and when you do, you can always look for new remote opportunities, or, if your job is unable to telecommute or you're unable to find employment, like many of the folks I spoke to, you can always do some consulting or freelancing.

Consulting

Consulting is exactly like remote work, except you have no idea where you're working tomorrow, and you have to actively solicit employment. For the purposes of brevity, we'll consider contract game development, freelancing, and consulting to be under one umbrella.

Step one will be to make sure you didn't sign a heinous noncompete agreement with your previous employer, or if you did, to legally challenge it. One of the better-kept secrets in the games industry is that vicious noncompetes and aggressively worded employment exclusivity agreements are almost completely unenforceable in court. In some states and countries, noncompete agreements are in fact *completely illegal*. Please don't take this as legal advice, but there are very few courts in the world that would hold up a restriction that completely destroys your career after voluntarily leaving your employment to seek a new opportunity. If you do review your hiring documents and find a big fat noncompete, it's best to consult a lawyer familiar with employment and intellectual property issues in your state or country immediately.

Once you've either found that you are free from a binding noncompete, or you have consulted a legal professional and decided that such a provision is an unenforceable, illegal overstep, you can feel free to seek new work. This can be as much work as your new venture, as it may involve advertising, soliciting, and ultimately trying to find work wherever it may be found.

As Nigel indicated in his interview, a great source of opportunity is your existing network. This does not mean poaching your former employer's customers in the event that you worked for a service provider—this portion of the noncompete often *is* enforceable—rather, it means consulting with your coworkers, peers, and friends to see who is looking for extra help on a project, or at their company, for a time-limited engagement. As Nigel indicated, you may literally be placing billboard trees on a hillside in an outdated engine for a year, but at least you'll be saving up cash and working toward your next big move. If, despite all of the above, you are still unable to find work in games in the interim, your next option is a second job outside of the games industry.

A Second Job

If the games industry isn't willing to let you work remotely and save up for your dream, the rest of the world absolutely is. Web development, marketing and PR, data entry and analysis, transcription, translation, art and asset contracting, and literally tens of thousands of other jobs are available to you either from your own living room or around the town you live in.

Some unfortunate truths pervade the games industry—we're very, very behind when it comes to labor standards. Where other companies have collective bargaining agreements, we have free bagels on Wednesday. Where others have arbitration and legal representation, we have rooms where you can cry privately. We have monthly controversies where companies take the side of their toxic fanbases over their own employees to the bitter end. We have brutal and penalizing nondisclosure and noncompete agreements, unenforceable though they may be. We have perpetual crunch, missed deadlines, layoff pizza parties, and escorts off of the premises by security without cause. I am elated to tell you that this is not normal.

As Ben elucidated in his interview, a quick switch to another industry, web development in his case, resulted in a normal 40-hour work week, flex time, vacation, retirement savings, a better salary, better benefits, a better work-life balance, and overall massive quality of life improvement. If you, like me, love the games industry and want to see it do better, perhaps the best strategy is to take advantage of another industry's progress, save cash, start your own business, and create the kind of company you'd like to see become a major player in games. Certainly the benefits, better pay, and free time can make this a more realistic possibility. After all, you're probably already used to working 80-hour weeks. Speaking of which, another possibility is to ...

Join a Startup

Chances are you're not the only person in the industry, or even in your office, thinking about making a change. Nigel and others found success in banding together and starting the company they wanted to work for. Investors and lenders sometimes call this "de-risking"—a one-person show is a lot scarier than having four or five skilled professionals taking a stab at it together. While I'm only slightly encouraging mutiny, probing your co-workers, colleagues, friends, and peers about their job satisfaction—gently—may reveal that there are skilled folks willing to make a change right under your nose.

You can also check out other companies that have recently started up in the industry. Steam publishes over ten thousand indie games per year, and among them are some real aces. Look to indie success stories, reach out, and see if someone with your skill set and industry experience would add value to their team. Additionally, you can attend local networking events hosted by your IGDA chapter or chamber of commerce to see if there are other games entrepreneurs in your area who need a partner.

The caveat here: if you're looking to forge it alone and create a world where you're the boss, joining a startup may dilute that authority. Additionally, startups often are an absolutely insane amount of work for very little—if any—pay. Make sure you're mentally and financially ready for those consequences.

Side Hustle

I like to tell people I'm a game dev, adjunct professor, and Lyft driver. As I put together Whitethorn Digital, I did everything from driving Lyft to Airbnb'ing my basement to building custom computer cases for people. There are myriad odd jobs you can do that bring in nontrivial income. All of the strategies that work in Los Angeles while struggling to afford your apartment, like working night shift at a bar after your day job, driving Lyft on the side, or renting a spare room, work in this situation as well.

Unfortunately, I can't give you much more advice than that. If you're good at something that is not your day job, like fixing cars, cleaning houses, sharpening knives, gardening, whatever, you can turn this into a reasonable side income that you do on your own schedule. This kind of option is particularly useful if you put yourself in a financially uncomfortable, but reasonably flexible situation, such as with joining a startup. You can also ...

Go Whole Hog

The classic entrepreneur's gamble is to go full bore into your new gig. If you're planning on making games, making a business for yourself, or starting some other enterprise, you can always apply for your own salary for a few years as part of the terms of your business loan. While this can provide significant stress, if you're supremely confident in your ability to turn a profit and have history and collateral, this may be an option for you.

One of the first steps is calculating your "runway." Given all the above information about trimming, saving, looking for side gigs, and more—you should be able to figure out exactly how much it costs to exist each month, how much you can reasonably bring in or have saved, and then determine how long you've got until you either need to find investment or start making serious money. By now, you should be very familiar with how long it takes to make a game, or part of a game if you're intending to start a contracting or consulting business.

Finally, if you're not absolutely sure yet, you might consider Ben's recommendation and try to make something small before you jump— noncompete permitting. If you're able, make a small game and sell it. Write a small book and see how it does. The effect of seeing a profit, even on a small, short, passion project is palpable, and often gives you the last little push needed to make the jump.

how do I get health care?

This question really only applies if you're one of my US readers. Other countries provide healthcare for entrepreneurs (and everyone else), which helps with creative endeavors like this. It's certainly easier to focus on getting your fledgling business off the ground and getting into the creative process without worrying about going bankrupt if you slip and break your ankle. Rant aside, you have a few options:

Healthcare.gov and the Healthcare Marketplace

Obamacare can help you, for now. Leaving your previous job in order to move to an entrepreneurial pursuit counts as a "qualifying event" under regulation, which means you probably also have COBRA as an option, although not a good one. If you happen to quit outside of open enrollment, the Healthcare Marketplace is the option for you. If you manage to time your departure from your current job with benefit open enrollment, even better. If you need to enroll, all of the information is at healthcare.gov. Plans are available across the price spectrum, but you can generally get in under $350 per person per month.

Remote Work

As discussed above, remote work confers a variety of benefits on employees, not the least of which is a salary. However, so long as you secure permanent full-time remote work, the company may also offer a benefit package. If you have no other healthcare option available, make this a bargaining piece when looking for remote jobs. Though many employers look for remote contractors who will not be offered healthcare or benefits, this is slowly changing.

Emigrate

While it might not sound like the best option, you could always explore leaving the country. Other than healthcare and salary, there are myriad other reasons why that might sound appealing right about now. This is a drastic measure, but there are dozens of other countries offering massive incentives to startup entrepreneurs abroad. Maybe it's time for you to have a new adventure? Many of the countries most interested in game developers set up booths at GDC. Drastic though it may be, the majority of the world provides tax incentives, healthcare, education, and other amenities that the US simply doesn't.

how do I fund my project?

This is a dilly of a question. A large number of successful startups are entirely self-funded. That is to say, the founders used their own money from savings and personal income to keep the business afloat until it became profitable. That has certainly been the case with Whitethorn Digital to date. However, there are a few avenues you can explore.

First, if you are intending to start a business in order to make games or provide services to the games industry, there are traditional business financing options. These are bank loans, and often require you to guarantee them with your personal income, retirement savings, or home. Beware—but then again, if you believe in yourself wholeheartedly, go for it.

Second, and this is more difficult, you can seek investments. This is referred to as startup fundraising, and an entire body of knowledge exists on the topic. Suffice to say, you will need to craft a very complete business plan, pitch, demo deck, and ideally, vertical slice of the product you are delivering. Once you have put together those materials, you will need to pitch to investors in the area, and if need be, nationally, and possibly even worldwide. On the upside, if you can secure an investor who is familiar with the games industry, you may secure both funding and an ideal mentor to help ensure your success—on the other hand, if you sign a deal with an investor who is not familiar with the industry, you may be rescuing a drowning swimmer. Tread carefully!

Third, more difficult still, is crowdfunding. Kickstarter, Patreon, IndieGogo, and the like, and more recently SeedInvest and StartEngine provide ideal methods to decentralize your sources of funding and allow your fans, friends, family, and people who believe in you to help fund your enterprise. The upside here is that, at least with traditional crowdfunding, the money comes without "strings." The downside is, of course, that it is a massive chore to raise funds in this way. You require marketing, pounding the pavement, and generally getting the word out that you are doing a campaign. In that way, crowdfunding is a bit like running for office. Instead of convincing one person your business works, you now have to convince a thousand.

Fourth and finally, if you have enough personal funds to get the game to a demo-ready state, you can always pitch to publishers, possibly even your own former employer. Nobody in the games industry is going to turn down a great deal, and if you make the next Minecraft but need another $250,000 to get it done, there are publishers aplenty willing to write you that check. Obviously this method is a bit of a "Hail Mary," since if you spend a quarter-million dollars making the demo and nobody bites, you're in a very difficult situation.

can I ever go back?

That depends entirely on how you left. If you drummed up the courage to walk in and told your boss, respectfully, that you'll be exploring new opportunities, and you left all of your work complete, you're probably fine. On the other hand, if you left snarky comments in the game's code, told anyone off, or left dog poop in the fridge, you're probably not fine. Many employers won't provide a reference, owing to the nondisclosure agreements that are prevalent in the industry. On the other hand, some are more than willing to do so; your experience will vary based on your employer.

The games industry is very small and very large, as you're probably aware. What you say and do will stay with you long after you leave your current company. To that end, it's probably best not to poach employees or customers, burn any bridges, or leave on negative terms. Leaving to start your own thing is exactly the same as, or slightly worse than, leaving to go to another company, from an employer's point of view. At least with another company, the possibility exists that tempting you with a large offer might have been what "made you leave." Forging off on your own plants the impression that you came up with this idea by yourself out of job dissatisfaction. Make sure to remind the employer that you're chasing a dream, not leaving because you're mad at the company—maybe tell a white lie.

I would encourage you not to let this question creep too far into your mind, though. The more you look over your shoulder, the less able you are to look to the horizon. For now, there will always be a games industry, and as long as there is a games industry, there will be a need for people to work in it. Assuming you've been working in it for some time, you have skills that are highly desired and in demand. If the need arose, the rest of this section notwithstanding, you could almost certainly return to the traditional industry.

what now ... ?

I wrote this short book as an encouragement piece. I want everyone in games to realize that they've made it, that their childhood dreams of getting their names in a video game credit list were valid, and that they've done good work. None of us had a dream of working ourselves to death or doing something we loathe. I'd like you all to know that no matter how many hours spent crunching, the number of layoffs you've faced, or the monetization loops you've had to work on and endure, you haven't done anything wrong. The fact that the games industry continues to suffer from basic labor and quality of life issues, that games consistently go over scope and over budget, and that employers continue to take advantage of the "dream job" has nothing to do with any action you've ever taken.

As you've seen in the interviews, every one of these accomplished game developers has faced some kind of hardship in pursuit of their dream of working in this industry. Whether that's nearly dying at the wheel, working a restaurant job dejected at not "making it," or growing tired of the executive-corporate-meeting-soup that can pervade some larger companies, every last one of us got into this thinking we were living our dream, and each of us was equally in for a rude awakening. I am here to tell you that these are the growing pains of a young industry, and it's up to you to lead by example.

Consider the film industry. The beginning of that industry, like ours, is ambiguous. It's somewhere around the turn of the twentieth century, argued to be 1897, 1900, and so on. After 30 years or so, the industry rapidly realized it was growing meteorically. Eventually, clubs and organizations started to form on the realization that actors were being worked to death in exchange for working in a glamorous industry. In the 1920s and 1930s, groups from various clubs and associations started to slowly organize, realizing that they were being given a raw deal. In 1933, the Screen Actors Guild was formed to represent the interests of workers in an exploding industry, that now, more than 80 years later, is still growing.

To that end, it would be impossible to talk about the future of the industry without mentioning the labor movement. Looking at the organization of the film industry and its unions, like SAG-AFTRA and the Teamsters, among others, we can see clear parallels to the current outmigration of talent in the games industry. Worker organization is starting to slowly take place in the form of @GameWorkersUnite and other industry labor organizations. We're not quite there yet, but we are making strides toward an organized labor force every day.

Like the film industry, the games industry is growing up. Depending on how you count, the games industry is barely 50 years old. The most iconic juggernauts of our entire industry are still making games. Shigeru Miyamoto, Hironobu Sakaguchi, Will Wright, John Carmack, Sid Meier, Michael Morhaime—at the time of writing, none of these folks are even old enough to retire, and yet they are the architects of our entire modern industry. As game developers, the future is ours to shape. Will this be an industry that crushes socially conscious views, rejects diversity and inclusion, and works employees to the bone, or will it evolve? That's up to us, right now. In every business, whether studio, contractor, middleware builder, or service provider, it's up to you to be an example for the industry to follow.

Hopefully this has given you some resources, points for consideration, and anchoring in the experience of others who have found success. If you're actively considering a move enough to pick up a book named *Breaking Out of the Games Industry*, there's a world of opportunity waiting for you. It's a great time to be part of the decentralization of the industry and to reshape what it will look like going into the future.

index